REVOLUTIONARY WAR GENEALOGY

by

George K. Schweitzer, Ph.D., Sc.D.
407 Ascot Court
Knoxville, TN 37923-5807

Wordprocessing by
Anne M. Smalley

ISBN 0-913857-04-1

TABLE OF CONTENTS

Chapter 1

THE REVOLUTIONARY WAR

1. Introduction

From 19 April 1775 until 03 September 1783 the American Revolutionary War was fought. On one side were thirteen rebelling American colonies of Great Britain, who were joined later in the war by France, Spain, and Holland. On the other side were the British along with their German mercenaries, a fair number of Loyalists (colonists who remained loyal to Great Britain), and several Indian groups. The thirteen colonies lay along the Atlantic seaboard of North America, occupying the approximate area of the present states of CT, DE, GA, MD, MA, NH, NJ, NY, NC, PA, RI, SC, and VA, plus land immediately to the west and the area which is now ME. Britain also held claim to the lands further to the west up to the MS River. The war was fought over this very large area extending essentially from the Atlantic Ocean to the MS River and from Canada to FL. The colonists were attempting to break away from Britain and to gain their independence, whereas the British were trying to subdue them and retain the territory in the British Empire. The war was terminated by the Treaty of Paris in 1783 which recognized an independent USA.

In 1775 the population of the thirteen colonies was almost 2,700,000. All in all, it is estimated that about 250,000 men fought for the colonies, and many more persons were involved directly or indirectly in support of the rebellion. Thus, over 9% (or about 1 out of 11) of the people were engaged as military participants and numerous others were involved in supportive action. Anyone, therefore, who had ancestors who were living in the colonies in 1775, has a high likelihood of being the descendant of one or more Revolutionary War veterans. For a war that was carried out over 200 years ago, a surprisingly large number of records has survived, even though highly destructive fires in 1800 and 1814 consumed many of those kept at a national level. Of the many records now available, a sizable fraction of them are fruitful sources of genealogical information. It is the purpose of this book to lead you to them and to assist you in extracting information on your ancestor(s) from them.

2. The background

In 1763, at the conclusion of the French and Indian War, Great Britain found herself the heir of two things: a vast territory in North America, and a large public debt. Prior to this time,

Britain had exercised a very loose colonial government and great laxity in the enforcement of trade, manufacturing, and commercial regulations. The colonies under this benign neglect had developed considerable self government and had not had to contend with strictly enforced commercial regulation and taxation. But in light of her large debt, Britain decided that the colonies needed to pay their share. So colonial administration was tightened up, more officials were sent in, further tax laws were passed, and all were rigorously enforced, even to denying the colonists jury trials and to making laws without permitting representation of the colonists. These policies caused colony congresses to express strong opposition and the colonists to organize local groups for protest, boycott, and, in a number of cases, riots and violent acts against British officials and property. British troops retaliated in several places, people were injured, and a few were killed. Local organizations throughout the colonies began to cooperate and political agitators induced them to begin to prepare for organized opposition against oppression.

In 1773, the whole growing movement against the British was accelerated by the granting of the trade monopoly to the British East India Company. Ships carrying tea were turned back at Boston, Philadelphia, and New York. Then on 16 December 1773, Bostonians threw a tea shipment overboard in their harbor. The British Parliament closed the harbor and sent four regiments to occupy the city. Town meetings and elective representation were forbidden in MA, and the news of the events quickly reached other colonies who pledged their support to MA. VA called for a Continental Congress which met in Philadelphia from 05 September to 26 October 1774. They denounced the treatment of MA, asserted their rights to liberty and property, and insisted that they be permitted to govern themselves through their colonial assemblies. The members of the Congress viewed themselves as still being loyal to Britain, but they claimed that their basic rights as British citizens were being denied. War clouds continued to gather as colonists armed themselves, gathered munitions and supplies, and activated their local militia units throughout the colonies. The scene was set for revolution, especially in and around Boston.

███████████████ On 18 April 1775, British Maj. Gen. Gage,
3. The beginnings commander of the 3000 troops in Boston,
             dispatched about 700 men under Lt. Col. Francis
███████████████ Smith to seize arms and munitions which had been
             collected by colonists at several places in the
countryside. Armed conflict occurred at Lexington and Concord, resulting

in 18 American casualties, but harassment of the British as they were driven back to Boston produced 273 casualties for them. Thousands of New England militia then gathered around Boston placing the city under seige. Shortly thereafter American Cols. Ethan Allen and Benedict Arnold led 300 other rebels to march into upper NY state to capture Ft. Ticonderoga on 10 May 1775 and Crown Point on 12 May 1775. On 25 May 1775 British Maj Gen. Gage received reinforcements under British Maj. Gens. Howe, Clinton, and Burgoyne. The British attacked 1500 entrenched Americans on Breed's and Bunker Hills just across from Boston on 17 June 1775. They finally drove the rebels from their city-threatening position, but not until they had lost over 1000 of the 2500 British soldiers involved.

Just before the battle at Breed's and Bunker Hills, the Second Continental Congress meeting on 14 June 1775 had voted to raise 20,000 troops, and the next day they chose George Washington as commander of the American forces. On 03 July 1775, Gen. Washington took charge of the New England army at Cambridge, MA. British Gen. Gage was replaced by Howe on 10 October 1775. An American army under Gen. Richard Montgomery invaded Canada and took St. John on 02 November 1775, then took Montreal on 13 November 1775, while Col. Arnold was marching a force across ME toward Quebec. The two groups met outside Quebec, but were beaten back when they attacked the city on 30 December 1775. In early March news was received of the defeat of a Loyalist group at Moore's Creek, NC by American militia on 27 February 1776. By this time, Americans besieging Boston had put artillery captured at Ticonderoga on the heights over the city, forcing the British to leave by ship on 17 March 1776 to go to Halifax, Nova Scotia. During that same Spring British forces sailed along the southern coasts attempting to rouse Loyalists against the new rebel governments in NC, SC, and GA. Their naval attack on Charleston, SC, on 28 June 1776, was unsuccessful, and little British action was seen in the South for the next two years. On 06 May 1776 the American forces which had remained in seige of Quebec withdrew because of sizable reinforcements which the British had sent in. And another invasion of Canada in June by American Gen. John Sullivan was forced back to Crown Point, NY, by British Gens. Carleton and Burgoyne. On 04 July 1776 the Continental Congress adopted the Declaration of Independence and hope of avoiding a larger and longer war had vanished.

4. The combatants It would seem to be folly for the colonies to attempt to split from Great Britain. Britain had a powerful navy, a trained and well-equipped army, a stable government, monetary backing, loyalists in the rebel colonies, loyal colonies north and south of the rebels, a population of about 9 million, a large merchant fleet, a well-developed industrial sector, and was at peace with all countries. The odds would appear to be strongly against the colonists who had essentially no naval forces, only ill-trained militiamen, no central government, no currency or credit, loyalists and neutralists in their midst, a population of less than 3 million, very few merchant vessels, quite scanty industrial works, few engineering and military experts, and no artillery. However, the rebelling colonists had plenty of at-hand manpower, short supply lines, they knew the country, could handle arms, were defending their strongly-held beliefs, could retreat to places beyond the reach of the British, and had the hope that Britain's old enemies (France, Spain, Holland) might help them by providing supplies, arms, and military experts. The British had to bring reinforcements from long distances, they were unfamiliar with the terrain, and their supply lines were exceptionally long, as were their communication lines. The British military forces consisted of British soldiers and sailors, Loyalists, German mercenaries, and Indians. At the peak of strength during the war, they had around 50,000 troops and 470 ships. The British strategy was to try to strangle the colonies through naval blockades and the seizure of the major port cities, then to divide the colonies by driving wedges of conquest between them which would permit subdual of the segments one by one. The American military forces consisted of the volunteer Continental Army and the militia, and later the French. The militia were organizations of civilians in local units which could be activated in crises. These units were sometimes gathered together as regional or state organizations, sometimes they acted independently, and at other times they fought along with the Continental Army. Usually the militia would fight in times of local invasion, but after the threat had passed, they would return to their farms and shops. The Continental Army had about 20,000 men at its peak and the navy numbered no more than 50 ships even though the colonists manned about 2000 privateers (privately-owned, armed ships). A total of about 250,000 men were involved, many fighting only for short periods of time, this producing sizable turnover, especially in the Continental Army.

The Americans set themselves to meet the British threats wherever they occurred. The Continental Army, reinforced with militiamen, met the British armies in the coastal regions where formalized warfare was usually fought. In the interior, the American militia did battle against Loyalists, British outposts, and Britain's Indian allies. The militia in the interior frequently employed guerilla tactics. Both the Continental Army and the militia operated in a more fluid manner than the British, now and again operating by surprise, ambush, rapid movement, delaying actions, and diversion. The British had success after success and yet saw their armies bled of men and supplies, while the defeated rebels sprang back. The British captured practically every major city in the colonies, and yet had little sense of having struck any blow, because there was no single vital strategic center to the rebel's efforts. There really was no American naval fleet since the colonists took to the sea in single ships, either privateers or vessels commissioned by the individual colonies or the Congress. These craft engaged in hit-and-run raids, seizing and plundering enemy ships, bringing supplies through the British blockade, and a few naval duels. All of the American effort could be sustained over a long period of time with the possibility of making the war so costly and wearing that the British would conclude it was no longer worth continuing.

5. The Colonial War

In the summer of 1776, the British laid plans to cut the colonies in two by sending Gen. Carleton from Quebec down the Lake Champlain-Hudson River route and sending Gen. Howe to capture New York City, then to go up the Hudson to meet Carleton. Gen. Carleton, after a delayed start, trouble marching through the wilderness, and a naval encounter with American ships on Lake Champlain, found winter setting in and returned to Canada. On 22 August 1776 British Gen. Howe landed 20,000 troops on Long Island with the aim of taking New York City which American Gen. Washington then occupied. On 27 August 1776 the British inflicted a disastrous defeat on 7000 American troops which Washington had placed on Brooklyn Heights. On the night of 29 August 1776, the remnant of the American contingent was ferried back across Manhattan. Then on 15 September 1776 the British landed on Manhattan and forced Washington northward to Harlem Heights where a successful stand was made. On 16 October 1776, Washington abandoned this position and moved further north to White Plains, NY, leaving about 2500 men at Ft. Washington, NY and sending about 300 to Ft. Lee, NJ, two forts astride the Hudson River. After a three-day stalemate battle at White Plains, NY, 28-31 October 1776, on 4-5 November Howe turned around and headed south for Ft. Washington which he captured on 16 November 1776. Ft. Lee was evacuated on 20 November 1776. The Americans retreated across NJ, and then into PA on 07 December 1776.

Figure 1. NORTHERN THEATER

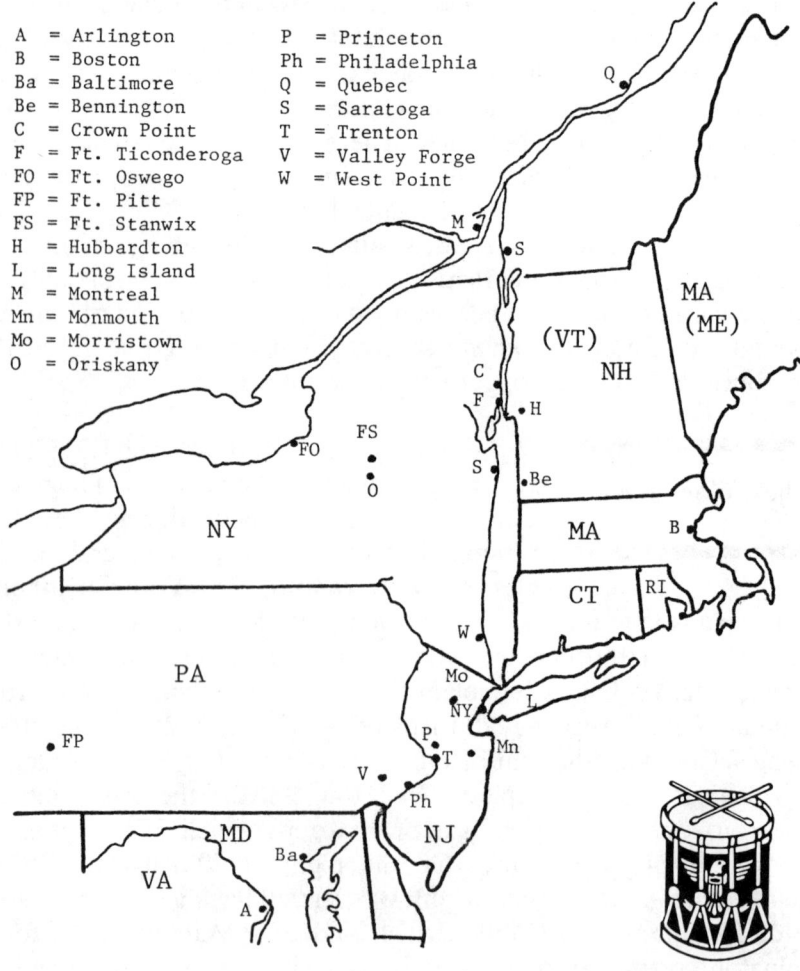

A = Arlington
B = Boston
Ba = Baltimore
Be = Bennington
C = Crown Point
F = Ft. Ticonderoga
FO = Ft. Oswego
FP = Ft. Pitt
FS = Ft. Stanwix
H = Hubbardton
L = Long Island
M = Montreal
Mn = Monmouth
Mo = Morristown
O = Oriskany

P = Princeton
Ph = Philadelphia
Q = Quebec
S = Saratoga
T = Trenton
V = Valley Forge
W = West Point

At this extremely low point, Washington made an unexpected move. Howe had quartered his forces for the winter in New York City and several NJ towns. Returning to NJ, Washington took captive the Germans at Trenton, NJ on 26 December 1776 and 8 days later routed the troops at Princeton, NJ. Washington then went into winter quarters at Morristown, NJ, and Howe withdrew his farthest outposts, bringing all of his army in near to NY City.

British plans for 1777 again involved attempts to split the colonies with two invasions from Canada and a northwestward movement by Gen. Howe from New York City. For some reason Howe began to move toward Philadelphia instead, and as soon as Washington recognized it, he started his army in that direction. On 25 August 1777, the British boats began to debark troops at the head of Chesapeake Bay, south of Philadelphia. Washington met them at Brandywine Creek on 11 September where he was defeated, permitting Howe to occupy Philadelphia. North of Philadelphia at Germantown Howe established a troop concentration. On 04 October 1777 Washington went into winter quarters at Valley Forge, about 20 miles northwest of Philadelphia. However, while these defeats were occurring in PA, an astonishing American victory was going on in NY.

In June 1776 Gen. Burgoyne started south from Canada with almost 8000 troops proceeding along the Lake Champlain-Hudson River route. Slightly later, in July, Lt. Col. St. Leger with 1700 men started out from Oswego to push down the Mohawk Valley and join Burgoyne. On 05 July 1777 Burgoyne took Ft. Ticonderoga, but St. Leger suffered heavy losses at Oriskany on 06 August 1777, and had to return to Canada when many of his Indian troops deserted him on the appearance of American reinforcements. Burgoyne dispatched a large group of Germans to capture food and horses from Bennington, VT, but they were decimated on 15 August 1777 by New England militia. Proceeding on south, Burgoyne arrived at Bemis Heights, NY, where American Gen. Gates and his Northern Army were entrenched. He made two powerful attacks on them, one 19 September 1777 and the other 07 October 1777, and was repulsed with heavy losses both times. With his army shattered and surrounded, and with no help in sight, Burgoyne surrendered his large force at Saratoga, NY, on 17 October 1777. The news of this defeat brought France to ally herself with the Americans against the British on 06 February 1778. Thus, what had been a colonial war now took on international proportions.

—————————————— In May 1778 British Gen. Howe resigned and
6. The expanded war was replaced by Gen. Clinton who was ordered
to leave Philadelphia and move his forces to
—————————————— New York City. Washington pursued him and
the two armies clashed at Monmouth, NJ on 28
June 1778, the outcome being indecisive. This battle marked the failure
of Britain to subdue the northern states, and large military operations in
that area were now at an end. Washington followed Clinton to New York
City and spent the next three years observing the British from positions
just outside the city. The war now moved to the west and the south.

In 1778, George Rogers Clark, responding to British-instigated Indian
threats to KY settlers, subdued several enemy-controlled towns and
settlements in the area that is now IN and IL. In 1776, the Cherokee of
the lower south were defeated several times by militia but still remained
troublesome. Gen. John Sullivan was dispatched to western NY by
Washington where he broke the power of the Iroquois by laying waste
many tribal villages during May-November 1779. Even so, neither the
British nor the Americans had gotten the upper hand on the frontier. The
war in the west continued to seesaw back and forth as Loyalists, Indians,
settlers, and patriot militia clashed again and again.

Failing to prevail in the north, the British shifted their resources to the
south where they believed they had strong Loyalist support. In November
1778 Clinton sent 3500 troops to join Gen. Prevost who was coming up
from FL. This British army met and defeated American Gen. Robert
Howe on 29 December 1778 as he attempted to defend Savannah, GA.
By the middle of February 1779 most of GA had been taken by the
British. American Gen. Lincoln with over 6000 men tried to retake GA
but did not succeed. He did, however, prevent a British takeover of
Charleston in May 1779. In September the French fleet and 4000 French
troops joined Gen. Lincoln in an effort to retake Savannah, GA, during
October 1779, but they were savagely repulsed and abandoned the action.

In February 1780, British Gen. Clinton came from New York to SC
with almost 9000 soldiers, and soon laid seige to Charleston, SC. On 12
May 1790 American Gen. Lincoln surrendered the city, over 300 cannon,
and over 5000 troops. Gen. Clinton then returned to New York leaving
Gen. Cornwallis in command of the British forces, who were to hold GA
and SC. Many people swore loyalty to the British King and Loyalists
began to attack those who did not, but resistance was kept alive by guerilla
raids, especially in the interior. By August 1780, American Gen. Gates

Figure 2. SOUTHERN THEATER

C   = Charleston
Ca = Camden
CB = Chesapeake Bay
Co = Cowpens
E   = Eutaw Springs
G   = Guilford C.H.
H   = Hobkirk s Hill
K   = Kings Mountain
N   = Ninety Six
P   = Petersburg
S   = Savannah
W   = Wilmington
Y   = Yorktown

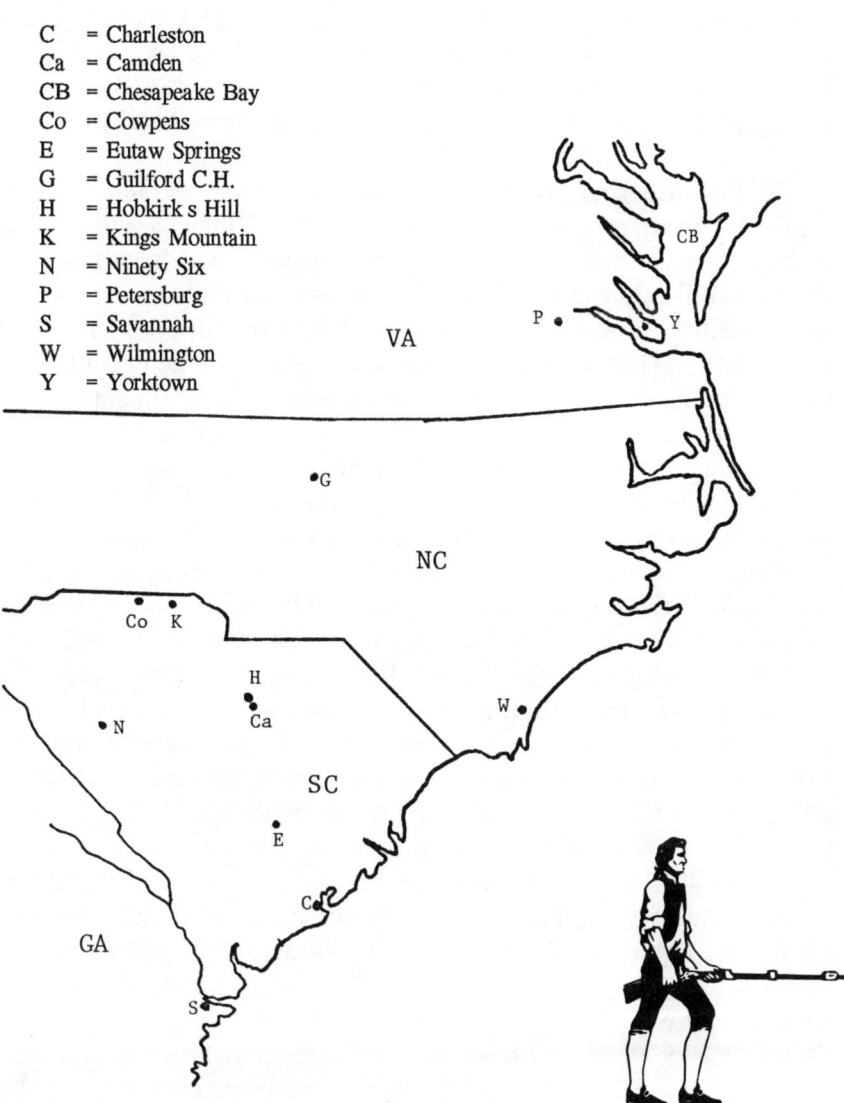

had assembled over 3000 troops, with which he invaded SC. He met Gen. Cornwallis at Camden, SC, on 16 August 1780 and was badly beaten. Cornwallis now moved into NC, where 1100 Loyalist soldiers headed east to join him. These Loyalists were surrounded on 07 October 1780 by 900 frontier riflemen who destroyed the contingent. This brought Cornwallis to return to Camden, SC, where in January 1781, he received 2500 more troops. When Cornwallis learned that British Gen. Benedict Arnold had invaded VA, he decided to push north through NC into VA to meet him.

As Cornwallis moved northward, he met American Gen. Greene, who sent his newly-raised troops first one way then another, inducing Cornwallis into a series of ineffective pursuits which baffled him and weakened his men. Gen. Greene sent his subordinate Gen. Morgan off to the southwest and Cornwallis dispatched Col. Tarleton with 1000 men in pursuit. Tarleton suffered a massive defeat when he caught Greene at Cowpens, SC, on 17 January 1781. American Gen. Greene now retreated across NC and VA, drawing the pursuing Cornwallis after him, lengthening the British supply lines greatly. Greene then challenged Cornwallis to do battle at Guilford Courthouse, NC, and Cornwallis accepted, where the two forces fought to a draw on 15 March 1781. The weakened British limped southeastward to Wilmington, NC, and Greene and his American troops turned south. Greene moved into SC where British Gen. Rawdon waited for him with 8000 soldiers who defeated him at Hobkirk's Hill on 25 April 1781. But, as happened with Cornwallis, the battle cost Rawdon so many men and supplies that he had to retreat. Patriot forces were now recapturing many British posts in SC and GA. By July 1781, the British held only Savannah and Charleston. When Greene advanced on Charleston, he was met by British Col. Stuart at Eutaw Springs, SC, where he was defeated, but again, Stuart's losses were very high, over 40%. From this time on, the British sat isolated and helpless in Charleston, SC, and Savannah, GA, surrounded by American patriots. No further fighting took place in the south except for guerilla action and hit-and-run raids.

7. The conclusion

Cornwallis left Wilmington, NC, and marched into VA in late April 1781 to meet Arnold on 20 May 1781 at Petersburg, VA. By August 1781 he had established his base at Yorktown, VA. On 30 August 1781 Adm. de Grasse moved a 28-battleship French fleet into Chesapeake Bay, thereby blockading the town by sea. The French Gen. de Rochambeau placed his troops under Washington's command and the combined French-American army moved out toward VA. A challenge to the French fleet was delivered on 05 September 1781 by a British naval force, but the British did not prevail and returned to New York City. On 28 September 1781, the 17000-man army under Washington surrounded Yorktown and began to attack on 06 October 1781. After intense artillery bombardment, Cornwallis surrendered his 8000 troops on 19 October 1781. Clinton, who was coming to Cornwallis' rescue with 7000 soldiers aboard a British fleet, turned back when he heard of the surrender.

From this point on, there was no major fighting, the Yorktown surrender serving to convince the British to abandon the war. Occasional fighting on a relatively small scale continued for about a year, principally in the south and west, but both sides set themselves mainly to wait for the diplomats to work out the peace agreement. Washington took his army back north to take up his watch over New York City, and the French troops sailed to the West Indies and Newport, RI, then in late 1782 returned to France. In the spring of 1782 the British commander Clinton was replaced by Carleton who ordered the evacuation of Savannah, GA, and Charleston, SC. This left the British in possession of only New York City as of the end of 1782.

On 30 November 1782, a preliminary peace treaty was signed. It acknowledged American independence and relinquished all the land between the Atlantic Ocean and the MS River and between Canada and Northern FL to the new country. The final treaty was signed in Paris on 03 September 1783, and the war was officially over. Washington made his farewell address to the army on 02 November 1783 and on the following day Congress pronounced the army disbanded. On 25 November 1783 the British left New York City, Washington resigned on 23 December 1783, and Congress ratified the peace treaty on 14 January 1784.

8. Recommended reading

The above account of the Revolutionary War is only a brief outline, meant simply to acquaint you with the general progress of the conflict. It mentions only the major battles, many others being fought in between the chief encounters. Should you want to do more detailed reading which will strongly enhance your understanding of your ancestor and your search for his records, it is recommended that you begin with two or three short treatments. Suitable materials for this include:

___ R. E. Evans, THE WAR OF AMERICAN INDEPENDENCE, Cambridge, New York, NY, 1976, 48 pages.

___ C. C. Calkins, THE STORY OF AMERICA, Readers Digest, Pleasantville, NY, 1975, pp. 25-47.

___ D. Higginbotham in ACADEMIC AMERICAN ENCYCLOPEDIA, Arete, Princeton, NJ, volume 1, pp. 353-65.

___ M. Jensen in COLLIER'S ENCYCLOPEDIA, Macmillan, New York, NY, 1980, volume 2, pp. 78-94.

___ P. C. Bowers, Jr., in ENCYCLOPEDIA AMERICANA, Americana Corp., Danbury, CT, 1979, volume 1, pp. 714-733h.

___ B. A. Weisberger, FAMILY ENCYCLOPEDIA OF AMERICAN HISTORY, Readers Digest, Pleasantville, NY, 1975, pp. 942-8.

___ R. B. Morris, editor, ENCYCLOPEDIA OF AMERICAN HISTORY, Harper & Row, New York, NY, 1976, pp. 96-134.

___ C. D. Linton, THE BICENTENNIAL ALMANAC, Nelson, New York, NY, 1975, pp. 18-35.

___ M. B. Grosvenor, AMERICA'S HISTORYLANDS, National Geographic, Washington, DC, 1967, pp. 177-263.

___ R. W. Coakley and S. Conn, THE WAR OF THE AMERICAN REVOLUTION, Center of Military History, US Army, Washington, DC, 1975, pp. 1-83.

Following these short discussions, if you wish you may go further by delving into one or more of the better one-volumed treatments of the American Revolution. Recommended are:

___ R. M. Ketchum, THE AMERICAN HERITAGE BOOK OF THE REVOLUTION, American Heritage, New York, NY, 1958.

___ I. Wernstein, 1776: THE ADVENTURE OF THE AMERICAN REVOLUTION, Cooper Square, New York, NY, 1962.

___ R. Furneaux, THE PICTORIAL HISTORY OF THE AMERICAN REVOLUTION, Ferguson, Chicago, IL, 1973.

___ R. B. Morris, THE MAKING OF A NATION, Time, New York, NY, 1963.

___ B. McDowell, THE REVOLUTIONARY WAR, National Geographic Society, Washington, DC, 1967.

___ W. J. Casey, WHERE & HOW THE WAR WAS FOUGHT, Morrow, New York, NY, 1976.

___ J. R. Alden, A HISTORY OF THE AMERICAN REVOLUTION, Knopf, New York, NY, 1969.

___ P. MacKesy, THE WAR FOR AMERICA, Harvard Univ. Press, Cambridge, MA, 1964.

___ M. Smelcer, THE WINNING OF INDEPENDENCE, Quadrangle, Chicago, IL, 1972.

___D. Higginbotham, THE WAR OF AMERICAN INDEPENDENCE, Macmillan, New York, NY, 1971.

___J. C. Miller, THE TRIUMPH OF FREEDOM, 1775-83, Little, Brown, Boston, MA, 1948.

For those who care to go much deeper into Revolutionary War history or portions of it, several multi-volumed sets are available. Among them you will find:

___P. Smith, A NEW AGE NOW BEGINS, McGraw-Hill, New York, NY, 1976, 2 volumes.

___S. Stember, THE BICENTENNIAL GUIDE TO THE AMERICAN REVOLUTION, Dutton, New York, NY, 1974, 3 volumes.

___G. O. Trevelyan, THE AMERICAN REVOLUTION, Longmans, Green, New York, NY, 1899, 4 volumes.

Also to be recommended is a volume which summarizes each day's important military events throughout the entire period of the war:

___T. N. Dupuy and G. N. Hammerman, PEOPLE AND EVENTS OF THE AMERICAN REVOLUTION, Bowker, New York, NY, 1974.

And not to be overlooked is a one-volumed encyclopedia of the Revolutionary War. This is a reference book giving short articles on all aspects of the Revolution (military, political, diplomatic, leaders, battles, maps, etc.) plus references to further material:

___M. M. Boatner, III, ENCYCLOPEDIA OF THE AMERICAN REVOLUTION, McKay, New York, NY, 1966.

The most extensive bibliography of the War for American Independence is the following 2-volumed set:

___R. M. Gephart, REVOLUTIONARY AMERICA, 1763-89, A BIBLIOGRAPHY, Library of Congress, Washington, DC, 1984. 100,000 references to almost 15,000 publications.

Chapter 2

THE ARCHIVES

1. The original records

The American Revolution generated a tremendous volume of records. Fortunately a sizable portion of them contain detailed genealogical information on more than 200,000 military participants who fought for American independence. In addition, the original records and records derived from them refer to wives and several million descendants of these veterans.

During the war, records included enlistment papers, muster rolls, pay rolls, attendance lists, regimental rosters, descriptive lists (detailed descriptions and vital data on participants), account books (on clothing, weapons, and rations issued), oaths of allegiance, and discharge papers. The records contain items such as name, rank, date, organization, enlistment date, term of service, promotions, reasons for absence (illness, wounded, death, furlough, discharged), birth place and date, place of civilian residence, civilian occupation, height, age, color of eyes and hair, and sometimes a signature. Rarely will all of these be available for a given soldier, sailor, or marine, but many will usually be.

In addition to the above, there were regimental orderly books (records of the orders given regiments by superior officers), communications between commanding officers (campaign plans, orders to lower officers, battle reports, lists of wounded and killed), lists of deserters, lists of prisoners, lists of enlistment expirations, petitions to their superior officers (for appointments, promotions, resignations), and records of the cities, counties, state legislatures, and the Continental Congress. Quite a number of the participants kept diaries or journals and wrote letters which have survived. Very recently the existence of extensive British records on the rebelling colonists (especially prisoners) have begun to be available.

After the war, even more records were generated. Many of the participants in the conflict had been promised land (called bounty land) for their service, many had been awarded bonus pay, and many were owed back pay. A large number of civilians were also owed money for service or supplies they provided to the military forces. The civilians and the veterans or their heirs filed claims for these debts with the state or national legislatures, the claims were acted upon, and payment records were kept. In addition, following the end of the war, pensions were awarded to veterans, their wives, and/or their heirs. These actions generated pension applications to the states and the federal government, decisions on the applications, pension payments, pension alterations as the laws were changed, and pension terminations. Pension applications can be of extreme value genealogically since they often provide the rank, state, military unit, dates of enlistment and discharge, birth date and place, amount of pension, places of residence to which the pension was sent, soldier's proof of military service, names of his officers, battle descriptions, property owned, date of death, widow's birth date and place, marriage date, names and birth dates of children, death date and place of widow, and affidavits of acquaintances, officials, and fellow soldiers. Applicants often went into considerable detail regarding their war experiences as they attempted to give proof of their service. Again, large volumes of records were involved. Such was also the case with bounty land applications. As you can imagine, some veterans made speeches, wrote articles, or even composed books describing their wartime adventures. A fair number of these are also available and often contain useful information on many persons who were in the same organization as the writer.

Most of the original records mentioned above are to be found in the National Archives in Washington, DC, in the State Archives of the original thirteen states, in university and private archives in those states, in a few archives in other states, in city and county records, and in French archives. The major ones of these records will be discussed in this chapter, and you will be told exactly how to find those relating to your Revolutionary War ancestor. Others will be treated in chapters to follow.

━━━━━━━━━━━━━━━━━

2. The initial approach

━━━━━━━━━━━━━━━━━

The very first thing you need to do is to write to the National Archives and ask them for three copies of Form NATF-80. This form will permit you to tap many of the vast record resources of the large collection there in Washington, DC. You should interrupt your reading and do this right now because the Archives is often slow in responding due to its heavy work load. The address is:

___Reference Service Branch (NNIR), National Archives, Washington, DC 20408.

Now that you have sent for your NATF-80 forms, you need to make a thorough preliminary survey. For every ancestor that you have traced to the 1775-83 time span, you should entertain the possibility that he gave military or civilian service in the war or that she married a serviceman or gave civilian service herself. Any person who was 16 years of age or older in 1783 is a live possibility.

The preliminary survey requires that you go to a fairly good genealogical library or that you hire a researcher at such a library to do the work for you. (A list of many such libraries will be found in section 1 of Chapter 3.) A cost of no more than $12 should be involved. In a good genealogical library, there will be located several published volumes which list large numbers of Revolutionary War participants. These include:

__National DAR, DAR PATRIOT INDEX, CENTENNIAL EDITION, The Society, Washington, DC, 1994, 31 volumes. [Over 140,000 names.]

__US Pay Department, War Department, REGISTER OF CERTIFI-CATES ISSUED BY JOHN PIERCE TO OFFICERS AND SOL-DIERS OF THE CONTINENTAL ARMY, Genealogical Publishing Co., Baltimore, MD, 1973. [Over 93,000 names.]

__National Genealogical Society, INDEX OF REVOLUTIONARY WAR PENSION APPLICATIONS IN THE NATIONAL ARCHIVES, The Society, Washington, DC, 1976. [About 80,000 entries.]

__F. Rider, editor, THE AMERICAN GENEALOGICAL-BIO-GRAPHICAL INDEX, Godfrey Memorial Library, Middletown, CT, 1952-81, volumes 1-, two series. [Over 80,000 Revolutionary War listings, volumes 1-180 in 2nd series now completed, more to come.]

You or your hired researcher should look for your ancestor in all four of these publications. It would be exceptionally helpful if you know or strongly suspect the state in which your ancestor lived. If he or she was actively involved in the war, your chances of finding him/her are quite high.

If you locate your ancestor, then fill out three Forms NATF-80 with as much data as you can, check the box on one asking for Military Service Records, on another for Pension Records, and on another for Bounty Land Records, write across the top of each form in red ink that you want the complete contents of the files, and mail the forms to the National Archives. Then, you'll simply have to be patient. As mentioned above, the Archives staff is very busy, and as long as three months may be required for a reply. When it does come, it will be a bill for their work, and when they receive payment, your material will be sent. If you don't want to wait on the Archives staff, you can hire a researcher in Washing-ton, DC, to go to the Archives and do the work for you. Even if you do not locate your ancestor in the four publications mentioned above, you should submit his name. The reason for this is that the National Archives indexes are more comprehensive than those of the publications.

With this bit of initial work done, and let's hope successfully, you will have just started getting Revolutionary War data on your veteran and his family. Succeeding sections and chapters will tell you how to search for a great deal more information.

If your search of the four basic volumes is negative, and if your NATF-80 Forms come back negative, there is still a possibility that your ancestor served. Your best hope of finding him is in various state and local records. This is because state and local records list Revolutionary War participants who are not mentioned in the national records. You will be told how to make these state and local searches in sections 4 and 6 of this chapter, sections 1-9 of Chapter 4, and sections 1-3 of Chapter 5.

3. The National Archives

The US National Archives, located at Pennsylvania Avenue between 7th and 9th Streets, NW, Washington, DC 20408, has the largest collection of Revolutionary War documents of any record repository. The keys to many of their vast resources reside in a set of five indexes, three of them being:

___National Archives, GENERAL INDEX TO COMPILED SERVICE RECORDS OF REVOLUTIONARY WAR SOLDIERS, The Archives, Washington, DC, Microfilm Publication M860, 58 rolls. Also available in printed form as V. White, INDEX TO REVOLUTIONARY WAR SERVICE RECORDS, National Historical Publishing Co., Waynesboro, TN, 1994, 4 volumes.

___National Archives, INDEX TO COMPILED SERVICE RECORDS OF AMERICAN NAVAL PERSONNEL DURING THE REVOLUTIONARY WAR, The Archives, Washington, DC, Microfilm Publication M879, 1 roll. [Also includes Marines.] Included in the printed volume by V. White, INDEX TO REVOLUTIONARY WAR SERVICE RECORDS, National Historical Publishing Co., Waynesboro, TN, 1994, 4 volumes.

___National Genealogical Society, INDEX OF REVOLUTIONARY WAR PENSION APPLICATIONS IN THE NATIONAL ARCHIVES, The Society, Washington, DC, 1976. [Also includes bounty land applications.]

These three indexes are the ones the personnel at the National Archives will examine when you submit Form NATF-80. The indexes will lead them to the Compiled Service Records, the Pension Records, and the Bounty Land Records (if the latter two were given). You will receive copies of what they find (or what your hired researcher will find). The copies will have been made from the Compiled Service Records of Soldiers (National Archives Microfilm Publication M881, 1097 rolls) or the Compiled Service Records of Naval Personnel (National Archives Microfilm Publication M880, 4 rolls), Selected Records from Revolutionary War Pension and Bounty Land Applications (National Archives Microfilm Publication M805, 898 rolls), and the Revolutionary War Pension and Bounty Land Application Files (National Archives Microfilm Publication M804, 2670 rolls). The selected records have been abstracted in two sets of published volumes:

___ V. White, GENEALOGICAL ABSTRACTS OF REVOLUTIONARY WAR PENSION FILES, National Historical Publishing Co., Waynesboro, TN, 1993, 4 volumes. Almost 400,000 entries.

___ C. Edmondson, REVOLUTIONARY WAR PERIOD BIBLE, FAMILY, AND MARRIAGE RECORDS GLEANED FROM PENSION APPLICATIONS, The Author, Dallas, TX, many volumes.

There are two other indexes which can often lead to sizable additional information on your ancestor. One of them, however, only applies to naval personnel. These are:

___ National Archives, SPECIAL INDEX TO NUMBERED RECORDS IN THE WAR DEPARTMENT COLLECTION OF REVOLUTIONARY WAR RECORDS, The Archives, Washington, DC, Microfilm Publication M847, 39 rolls.

___ National Archives, CARD INDEX TO THE AREA FILE OF THE NAVAL RECORDS COLLECTIONS, 1775-1910, The Archives, Washington, DC.

The first index will lead you or your hired researcher to records in the Numbered Record Books (National Archives Microfilm Publication M853, 41 rolls) and in the Miscellaneous Numbered Records (National Archives Microfilm Publication M859, 125 rolls). In these two series, there are to be found many data which are not included in the compiled service records (lists of soldiers from state sources, orderly books, delayed pay certificates, account books, official correspondence, petitions, personal letters, and numerous other items). In the second index, there are references to both persons and ships in the Area File of Naval Records (National Archives Microfilm Publication M625, 414 rolls, but only 17 rolls pertaining to the Revolutionary War). A mail inquiry to the National Archives will bring a reply regarding whether your ancestor appears in either or both of these indexes. Be sure and ask them the cost of copying the records if they locate any.

All of the above microfilms (M804, M805, M847, M853, M859, M860, M879, M880, M881) except M625 are available at the Family History Library of the Genealogical Society of UT in Salt Lake City, and may be borrowed through their hundreds of branches throughout the US (see list in section 1, Chapter 3). The major microfilm index (M860) and the service record (M881) and pension and bounty land application (M804) microfilms are available in the regional branches of the National Archives (Atlanta, Boston, Chicago, Denver, Fort Worth, Kansas City, Los Angeles, New York, Philadelphia, San Francisco, Seattle). They (M860, M851, M804) may all be borrowed for you for a small fee by your local library from AGLL, PO Box 244, Bountiful, UT 84010. Or you can borrow them directly from AGLL after joining their lending network. The major microfilms (M860, M881, M804) are also often in the holdings of state libraries and large genealogical libraries. By using these facilities, you can examine the major records without writing the National Archives and submitting forms NATF-80. The two sets of books by V. White (Service Record Index, Pension Application Abstracts) are available in many large genealogical libraries.

If your ancestral veteran was an officer, it might be well to search for any petition he may have filed for his officer's commission, a promotion, or for permission to resign (which he had to have). If your ancestor was an officer or an enlisted man, he may have had pension or claim or petition dealings with the federal authorities. The indexes to the following records should be consulted, the index for the second being at the Library of Congress.

___National Archives, PAPERS OF THE CONTINENTAL CONGRESS, 1774-89, The Archives, Microfilm Publication M247, 204 rolls; also MISCELLANEOUS PAPERS OF THE CONTINENTAL CONGRESS, 1774-89, The Archives, Microfilm Publication M332, 10 rolls; both indexed in J. P. Butler, INDEX TO THE PAPERS OF THE CONTINENTAL CONGRESS, National Archives and Records Service, Washington, DC, 1978, 5 volumes.

___Library of Congress, THE GEORGE WASHINGTON PAPERS, The Library, Washington, DC.

___DIGESTED SUMMARY AND ALPHABETICAL LIST OF PRIVATE CLAIMS PRESENTED TO THE HOUSE OF REPRESENTATIVES, 1st-31st CONGRESS, Genealogical Publ. Co., Baltimore, MD, 1970, leads to detailed records in Record Group 233,

National Archives. [Over 60,000 persons who filed claims.]
Again, letters may be addressed to the National Archives and the Library of Congress asking them to check the indexes and quote you a price for copying any materials they may find. Or you may hire a researcher.

More details on the above sources and a number of other sources in the National Archives will be found in the two following publications:
___M. E. Deutrich and H. H. Wehmann, PRELIMINARY INVENTORY OF THE WAR DEPARTMENT COLLECTION OF REVOLUTIONARY WAR RECORDS, No. 144, National Archives, Washington, DC, 1970.
___National Archives, GUIDE TO GENEALOGICAL RESEARCH IN THE NATIONAL ARCHIVES, The Archives, Washington, DC, 1982. [See Revolutionary War in the index.]
In these publications you will find further items such as naval affairs, commissions of privateers, records of supplies, records of British ship seizures, claims of CT Revolutionary War invalids, MA pension applications, Revolutionary War account books and journals, diplomatic missions, US war debts, lottery journals, loans to the US, US interest payments, illustrations and drawings, naval orders and directories, correspondence regarding bounty land warrants, and pension correspondence.

---

4. State achives and repositories

The State Archives of the states arising from the 13 original colonies and those of several of the earlier additional states contain a wide variety of primary records. It is quite important for you to seek your ancestor in state records, since many persons who served in the Revolutionary War were not included in federal records. This is particularly true of those men who served in the militia. State records pertain largely to their own participants in the Revolutionary War. Many of the types of original records mentioned in section 1 of this chapter are likely to be found there. Once you have discovered the state under which your ancestor served, you should write the State Archives (or other designated repository) asking about available records and enclosing an SASE for their reply. Be certain that you ask about bounty land records, since many veterans received bounty land from the states rather than from the federal government. Also do not forget to ask about information on the military unit to which your ancestor belonged. The Archives will answer brief questions for you, but they are not staffed fully enough to undertake research in the records for you. Therefore, you might also ask them for a list of researchers whom you could hire to conduct a detailed investigation of the documents which could refer to your veteran.

A listing of pertinent State Archives or other pertinent repositories along with their addresses (and brief indications of their major holdings) follows:

___For AL,* AL Department of Archives and History, 624 Washington Avenue, Montgomery, AL 36130. Lists of resident veterans.

___For CT, CT State Library, 231 Capital Avenue, Hartford, CT 06106. Indexes, regimental rolls, pensioners, burial, commissions, confiscated estates, militia, prisoners, claims, petitions, taxes, registers, lists, societies, manuscripts.

___For DE, The Public Archives Commission, DE Hall of Records, Dover, DE 19901. Indexes, rolls, lists, registers, oaths of allegiance, pensions, petitions, commissions, treason charges, manuscripts.

___For GA, GA Department of Archives and History, 330 Capitol Ave., SE, Atlanta GA 30334. Militia, regimental returns, commissions, land lotteries, rosters, payrolls.

___For KY,* KY Department of Libraries and Archives, 300 Coffee Tree Road, Frankfort, KY 40602. Claims, land grants, lists, burials.

___For ME,* ME State Archives, Cultural Bldg., Augusta, ME 04333. Burials, pensions, bounty lands. Also see MA, because ME was part of MA during the Revolution.

___For MD, MD State Archives, 350 Rowe Blvd,, Annapolis, MD 21401. Indexes, lists, payrolls, muster rolls, pensions, oaths of fidelity, manuscripts.

___For MA, Military Records Section, Room 100, The Adjutant General's Office, Military Division, 100 Cambridge St., Boston, MA 02202. Rosters, rolls, orders, courts-martial, discharges. MA Archives, 220 Morrissey Blvd., Boston, MA 02125. Indexes, pensions, bounty lands, privateers, deserters, prisoners, rolls, lists, orders, discharges, militia, navy, bounties, enlistments

___For NH, NH State Archives, 71 South Fruit St., Concord, NH 03301. Rolls, rosters, indexes, courts-martial, enlistments, oaths, accounts, invalids, manuscripts.

___For NJ, NJ State Archives, 185 West State St., Trenton, NJ 08625. Forfeited estates, militia, pensions, service records, damages, Loyalists, officers.

___For NY, NY State Archives and NY State Library, Cultural Education Center, Empire State Plaza, Albany, NY 12230. Muster rolls, bounty land, pensions, indexes.

___For NC, NC State Archives, 109 East Jones St., Raleigh, NC 27601.

Returns, indexes, payrolls, service records, pensions, courts-martial, officers, accounts, muster rolls, manuscripts.

___For OH,* OH Historical Society, Archives-Library Division, 1982 Velma Ave., Columbus, OH 43211. VA Military District land recipients, burials, veterans, manuscripts.

___For PA, PA State Archives, Third and Forster Sts., Harrisburg, PA 17108. Indexes, militia, line troops, navy, pensions, accounts, payrolls, muster lists, claims, commissions, passes, forfeited estates, donation land, land patents.,

___For RI, RI State Archives, 337 Westminster St., Providence, RI 02903. Indexes, payrolls, muster rolls, pensioners, casualties, suspected persons, confiscated estates, accounts, burials, claims, manuscripts.

___For SC, SC Department of Archives and History, 1430 Senate St., Columbia, SC 29211. Indexes, accounts, claims, Loyalists, manuscripts.

___For TN,* Archives Section, TN State Library and Archives, 403 7th Ave., N., Nashville, TN 37219. Indexes, resident veterans, warrants for bounty land, manuscripts.

___For VT,* Department of Veterans' Affairs, Office of the Adjutant General, 120 State St., Montpelier, VT 05620. Burials, rolls.

___For VA, VA State Library and Archives, 12th and Capitol Sts., Richmond, VA 23219. Indexes, lists, returns, fines, rosters, bounty warrants, pensions, claims, impressed property, accounts, half-pay claims, state line, continental line, militia, muster rolls, Clark papers, KY militia, Loyalists, seamen, navy, OH land, manuscripts.

The states marked with an asterisk are those which were not among the original thirteen. All of them will have sizably fewer primary records than the original states.

In some states, sometimes the State Libraries and sometimes the State Historical Societies happen to function as record repositories as well as housing published materials. In addition, they sometimes will have card indexes to pertinent Revolutionary War listings. It is therefore advisable for you to write these organizations concerning records of your ancestor. Be sure to enclose a long SASE and make your inquiry brief, that is, simply ask them if they have any records on your veteran or on your veteran's military unit, and, if so, to quote you a price for providing copies, or if they cannot do this much work, to send you a listing of researchers.

A listing of those State Libraries and Historical Societies which have useful holdings along with their addresses follows:

___For CT, CT Historical Society, 1 Elizabeth St., Hartford, CT 06105. Muster rolls, accounts, payrolls, orderly books, naval officers.

___For DE, Historical Society of DE, 505 Market Street Mall, Wilmington, DE 19801. Manuscripts.

___For GA, GA Historical Society, 501 Whittaker St., Savannah, GA 31499. Manuscripts.

___For KY,* KY Department of Military Affairs, Military Records and Research Branch, 1121 Louisville Road, Frankfort, KY 40601. Burials, militia. National Society Sons of the American Revolution, 1000 South Fourth Street, Louisville, KY 40203. KY Historical Society Library, 200 Broadway, Frankfort, KY 40601.

___For ME,* ME Historical Society, 485 Congress St., Portland, ME 04111. Muster rolls, pensions, bounty land, claims, orderly books, manuscripts.

___For MD, MD Historical Society, 201 W. Monument St., Baltimore, MD 21201. Militia, accounts, county military records, manuscripts.

___For MA, MA Historical Society, 1154 Boylston St., Boston, MA 02215. Muster rolls, lists, orderly books, British military men, manuscripts.

___For MO,* MO Historical Society, 225 South Skinker Blvd., St. Louis, MO 63112. Manuscripts, SAR members.

___For NH, NH Historical Society, 30 Park St., Concord, NH 03301. Burials, manuscripts.

___For NJ, NJ Historical Society, 230 Broadway, Newark, NJ 07104. Manuscripts. NJ Historical Commission, 113 West State St., Trenton, NJ 08625. Manuscripts.

___For NY, NY Historical Society, 170 Central Park West at 77th St., New York, NY 10024. Manuscripts.

___For NC, NC State Library, 109 E. Jones St., Raleigh, NC 27611.

___For OH,* Western Reserve Historical Society Library, 10825 East Blvd., Cleveland, OH 44106. Manuscripts.

___For PA, Historical Society of PA, 1300 Locust St., Philadelphia, PA 19107. Manuscripts. PA State Library, Education Bldg., Walnut and Commonwealth Aves., Harrisburg, PA 17126.

___For RI, The Library of the RI Historical Society, 121 Hope St., Providence, RI 02906. Burials, manuscripts.

___For SC, SC Historical Society, 100 Meeting St., Charleston, SC 29201. Manuscripts.

___For VT,* VT Historical Society Library, State Administration Bldg., 109 State St., Montpelier, VT 05602.

___For VA, VA Historical Society Library, PO Box 7311, Richmond, VA 23211. Manuscripts.

The asterisks again indicate states which were not among the original thirteen. Thus, their repositories will hold less information on the Revolutionary War and its participants.

	A very important source for military historical material
5. The AMHI	is the US Army Military History Institute (AMHI) which is located at Carlisle Barracks, PA, just outside of Carlisle, PA.

This institute is the Army's official central repository for historical materials relating to the US Army. The holdings include several thousand volumes on the Revolutionary War, consisting of memoirs, diaries, documentary collections, rosters, papers of military personages, biographies, campaign accounts, battle descriptions, and numerous monographs dealing with special subjects. Much of this collection is listed in:

___J. L. Eakin, COLONIAL AMERICA AND THE WAR FOR INDEPENDENCE: A MILITARY HISTORY RESEARCH COLLECTION BIBLIOGRAPHY, Special Bibliographic Series No. 14, US Army Military History Institute, Carlisle Barracks, PA, 1976.

After you have done considerable research on your ancestor and have obtained data on him and his military unit, it may be helpful for you to visit or write the AMHI. Send the Institute your ancestor's name and his military unit, and ask them to see what they can find pertaining to his unit. Be patient because they often have a fairly good sized backlog, but you should receive an answer from them in several weeks. The address is:

___Reference Branch, The US Army Military History Institute, Carlisle Barracks, PA 17013.

The staff of the Institute cannot do extensive research but they will locate material for you, tell you what they have, and give you costs for making machine copies. They will also permit your local library to borrow books for you on interlibrary loan. If extensive research is called for, you will need to employ a professional researcher or visit the Institute yourself. They are open 8:00 am-4:30 pm, Mondays through Fridays, except Federal Holidays.

	In addition to the National Archives, the State
6. Other archives	Archives, and the AMHI, there are numerous other archives and manuscript repositories which have original Revolutionary War materials.

Many of these materials contain information on individual participants. It is possible that data on your ancestor or at least on his military companions or his officers or his military unit may be in them. Unfortunately, there is no short and sure way to locate the data. It is recommended that you delay your search of these other archives until you have made use of the published materials which are mentioned in Chapters 3 and 4, and which are much easier and quicker to find and employ. Then you can return to the more difficult and time-consuming archives search. What is required is a search among the various volumes which describe the holdings in these archives. Be sure to make good use of the indexes, especially being careful not to overlook ones which list individual names. Of course, the higher in rank your veteran was, the more likely you are to find him. As we will mention later, don't overlook materials relating to your ancestor's superior officers or to his military unit (company, regiment, brigade).

Your first examinations should be of several excellent volumes which list and give brief descriptions of archives and manuscript repositories in the US which have sizable holdings of Revolutionary War materials. When you locate places which look to be good possibilities for your ancestor, his officers, or his unit, send them an SASE, inquire about their holdings, and ask them about researchers you can hire (unless you can make a personal visit). The most useful reference volumes of this type are listed below. Most of them will be available in state, larger city, larger university, and larger genealogical libraries.

___National Historical Publications and Records Commission, DIRECTORY OF ARCHIVES AND MANUSCRIPT REPOSITORIES IN THE US, National Archives, Washington, DC, 1978. [See Revolutionary War on page 741 of index.]

___H. Cripe and D. Campbell, AMERICAN MANUSCRIPTS, 1763-1815, Scholarly Resources, Wilmington, DE, 1977.

___J. R. Sellers, G. W. Gawalt, P. H. Smith, and P. E. Van Ee, MANUSCRIPT SOURCES IN THE LIBRARY OF CONGRESS FOR RESEARCH OF THE AMERICAN REVOLUTION, Government Printing Office, Washington, DC, 1975.

___P. M. Hamer, A GUIDE TO ARCHIVES AND MANUSCRIPTS IN THE US, Yale University Press, New Haven, CT, 1961. [See Revolutionary War on page 872 of index.]

___US Library of Congress, NATIONAL UNION CATALOG OF MANUSCRIPT COLLECTIONS, Shoe String Press, Hamden, CT, 1959-. [Indexes of names, places, historical periods.] Be sure to use the accompanying collective name and subject indexes.

___W. S. Jenkins and L. A. Hamrich, A GUIDE TO THE MICROFILM COLLECTION OF EARLY STATE RECORDS, Library of Congress, Washington, DC, 1950, with SUPPLEMENT, 1951.

___N. B. Cuthbert, AMERICAN MANUSCRIPT COLLECTIONS IN THE HUNTINGTON LIBRARY FOR THE HISTORY OF THE 17TH AND 18TH CENTURIES, The Library, San Marino, CA, 1941.

___R. A. Billington, GUIDES TO AMERICAN HISTORY

MANUSCRIPT COLLECTIONS IN LIBRARIES OF THE US, Mississippi Valley Historical Review, volume 38, 1951-2, pp. 467-96.
___H. M. Forbes, NEW ENGLAND DIARIES, 1602-1800, The Author, Topfield, MA, 1923.
___C. N. Smith, FEDERAL LAND SERIES: A CALENDAR OF AR-CHIVAL MATERIALS ON THE LAND PATENTS ISSUED BY THE US, WITH NAME INDEXES, American Library Association, Chicago, IL, 1972-.
___C. H. Lincoln, NAVAL RECORDS OF THE AMERICAN REVOLUTION, Government Printing Office, Washington, DC, 1906.

The next move you need to make in your manuscript and document search is to look into archive guides for the general localities where your ancestor lived, enlisted, and fought. Again, when likely references are found, send an SASE, an inquiry, and ask about researchers (unless you can go personally). Among the better guides are the following. They will be a bit more difficult to locate, larger libraries in or near their areas being more likely to have them.
___In CT, J. Sylvester, CT ARCHIVES FOR THE REVOLUTIONARY WAR, 1763-1820.
___M. E. Baker, BIBLIOGRAPHY OF LISTS OF NEW ENGLAND SOLDIERS, New England Historical and Genealogical Register, volume 64 (1910) pp. 61-72, 128-35, 228-37, 327-36; volume 65 (1911) pp. 11-19, 151-60.
___In MD, A. J. M. Pedley, THE MANUSCRIPT COLLECTIONS OF THE MD HISTORICAL SOCIETY, The Society, Baltimore, MD, 1968.
___R. J. Cox, A CHECKLIST OF REVOLUTIONARY WAR MANUSCRIPT COLLECTIONS ACCESSIONED SINCE 1968, MD Historical Magazine, volume 71, 1976, pp. 252-63.
___MD Hall of Records Commission, CALENDAR OF MD STATE PAPERS, The Commission, Annapolis, MD, 1943-.
___MD Hall of Records Commission, CATALOG OF ARCHIVAL MATERIAL, The Commission, Publication No. 2, Annapolis, MD, 1942.
___In MA, Boston Public Library, MANUSCRIPTS OF THE AMERI-CAN REVOLUTION IN THE BOSTON PUBLIC LIBRARY, Hall, Boston, MA, 1968.
___Historical Records Survey, GUIDE TO DEPOSITORIES OF MANUSCRIPT COLLECTIONS IN MA, The Survey, Boston, MA, 1939.
___MA Historical Society, CATALOG OF MANUSCRIPTS OF THE

MA HISTORICAL SOCIETY, Hall, Boston, MA, 1969, 7 volumes.

___ J. Winsor, CALENDAR OF THE SPARKS MANUSCRIPTS IN HARVARD COLLEGE LIBRARY, The Library, Cambridge, MA, 1889.

___ See Baker reference under CT.

___ In NH, Historical Records Survey, GUIDE TO DEPOSITORIES OF MANUSCRIPT COLLECTIONS IN NH, The Survey, Manchester, NH, 1940.

___ See Baker reference under CT.

___ In NJ, A. P. Clark, THE MANUSCRIPT COLLECTIONS OF THE PRINCETON UNIVERSITY LIBRARY, Princeton University Press, Princeton, NJ, 1958.

___ Historical Records Survey, CALENDAR OF THE NJ STATE LIBRARY MANUSCRIPT COLLECTION, The Survey, Newark, NJ, 1939.

___ Historical Records Survey, GUIDE TO DEPOSITORIES OF MANUSCRIPT COLLECTIONS IN NJ, The Survey, Newark, NJ, 1941.

___ F. Shelley, A GUIDE TO THE MANUSCRIPT COLLECTION OF THE NJ HISTORICAL SOCIETY, The Society, Publication No. 11, Newark, NJ, 1957.

___ H. F. Smith, A GUIDE TO THE MANUSCRIPT COLLECTION OF THE RUTGERS UNIVERSITY LIBRARY, Rutgers University Press, New Brunswick, NJ, 1964.

___ B. W. Stewart and H. Mayer, A GUIDE TO THE MANUSCRIPT COLLECTION, MORRISTOWN NATIONAL HISTORICAL PARK, Morristown, NJ, 1964.

___ In NY, S. Bielinski, A GUIDE TO THE REVOLUTIONARY WAR MANUSCRIPTS IN THE NY STATE LIBRARY, NY American Revolution Bicentennial Committee, Albany, NY, 1976.

___ K. N. Mango, THE LONG ISLAND HISTORICAL SOCIETY CALENDAR OF MANUSCRIPTS, 1763-83, The Society, New York, NY, 1980.

___ A. J. Breton, A GUIDE TO THE MANUSCRIPT COLLECTION OF THE NY HISTORICAL SOCIETY, Greenwood, Westport, CT, 1972, 2 volumes.

___ E. B. Greene and R. B. Morris, A GUIDE TO THE PRINCIPAL SOURCES FOR EARLY AMERICAN HISTORY IN THE CITY OF NY, 1600-1800, Columbia University Press, New York, NY, 1953.

___ Historical Records Survey, GUIDE TO DEPOSITORIES OF MANUSCRIPT COLLECTIONS IN NY, The Survey, Albany, NY, 1941.

___NY Public Library, DICTIONARY CATALOG OF THE MANUSCRIPT DIVISION, Hall, Boston, MA, 1967, 2 volumes.

___E. M. Ruttenber, CATALOG OF MANUSCRIPTS AND RELICS IN WASHINGTON'S HEADQUARTERS, Newburgh, NY, 1890.

___NY Adjutant General's Office, CALENDAR OF NY COLONIAL MANUSCRIPTS, The Office, Albany, NY, 1864.

___In NC, S. S. Blosser and C. N. Wilson, Jr., THE SOUTHERN HISTORICAL COLLECTION: A GUIDE TO MANUSCRIPTS, University of NC Library, Chapel Hill, NC, 1970 with SUPPLEMENTARY GUIDE, University of NC Library, Chapel Hill, NC, 1976.

___B. G. Crabtree, GUIDE TO PRIVATE MANUSCRIPT COLLECTIONS IN THE NC STATE ARCHIVES, NC State Department of Archives and History, Raleigh, NC, 1964.

___Historical Records Survey, GUIDE TO DEPOSITORIES OF MANUSCRIPT COLLECTIONS IN NC, NC Historical Commission, Raleigh, NC, 1940.

___N. M. Tilley and N. L. Goodwin, GUIDE TO MANUSCRIPTS IN THE DUKE UNIVERSITY LIBRARY, Duke University Press, Durham, NC, 1947.

___In PA, W. J. Bell, Jr. and M. D. Smith, GUIDE TO THE ARCHIVES AND MANUSCRIPT COLLECTIONS OF THE AMERICAN PHILOSOPHICAL SOCIETY, Memoirs of the Society, volume 66, Philadelphia, PA, 1966.

___Historical Records Survey, GUIDE TO THE MANUSCRIPT COLLECTIONS OF THE HISTORICAL SOCIETY OF PA, The Society, Philadelphia, PA, 1949.

___PA Historical and Museum Commission, CATALOG OF THE MANUSCRIPT COLLECTION OF THE PA STATE ARCHIVES, The Commission, Harrisburg, PA, 1976.

___PA Historical and Museum Commission, PRELIMINARY GUIDE TO THE RESEARCH MATERIALS OF THE PA HISTORICAL AND MUSEUM COMMISSION, The Commission, Harrisburg, PA, 1959.

___Genealogical Society of PA, GENEALOGICAL MANUSCRIPT MATERIAL INDEX, The Society, Philadelphia, PA, 1964.

___DAR of PA, LOCATION OF UNPUBLISHED MANUSCRIPT MATERIAL, National Historical Magazine, March, 1940, pp. 33 ff.

___M. S. Eliot and S. K. Stevens, GUIDE TO DEPOSITORIES OF MANUSCRIPT COLLECTIONS IN PA, Bulletin 774, PA Historical Commission, Harrisburg, PA, 1939.

___H. H. Eddy and M. L. Simonetti, GUIDE TO THE PUBLISHED

ARCHIVES OF PA, Historical and Museum Commission, Harrisburg, PA, 1976.

___In RI, see Baker reference under CT.

___In SC, H. G. McCormick, A PROVISIONAL GUIDE TO THE MANUSCRIPTS IN THE SC HISTORICAL SOCIETY, SC Historical and Genealogical Magazine, volumes 45-48, 1944-7.

___In VA, VA Historical Society, CATALOG OF MANUSCRIPTS IN THE COLLECTION OF THE VA HISTORICAL SOCIETY, Jones, Richmond, VA, 1901.

___H. R. McIlwaine, THE REVOLUTIONARY WAR MATERIAL IN THE VA STATE LIBRARY, Virginia Magazine of History, volume 10, 1909, pp. 143-50.

___C. A. Flagg and W. O. Waters, VA'S SOLDIERS IN THE REVOLUTION: A BIBLIOGRAPHY, Virginia Magazine of History, volume 19, 1911, pp. 402-14; volume 20, 1912, pp. 52-68, 181-94, 267-81; volume 21, 1913, pp. 337-46; volume 22, 1914, pp. 57-67, 177-86.

___In ME, ME University, A REFERENCE LIST OF MANUSCRIPTS RELATING TO THE HISTORY OF ME, University of ME Studies, 2nd Series, No. 45, University of ME Press, 1938.

___In MI, H. H. Pecham, GUIDE TO MANUSCRIPT COLLECTIONS IN THE WILLIAM L. CLEMENTS LIBRARY, The Library, Ann Arbor, MI, 1942; Second Edition by W. S. Ewing, 1953.

___In WI, A. E. Smith, GUIDE TO MANUSCRIPTS OF THE WI HISTORICAL SOCIETY, The Society, Madison, WI, 1944; SUPPLEMENTS, 1956 and 1966.

Other archive references of value include:

___In CA, N. B. Cuthbert, AMERICAN MANUSCRIPT COLLECTIONS IN THE HUNTINGTON LIBRARY FOR THE HISTORY OF THE 17TH AND 18TH CENTURIES, The Library, San Marino, CA, 1941.

___For overseas archives, W. J. Koenig and S. L. Mayer, EUROPEAN MANUSCRIPT SOURCES FOR THE AMERICAN REVOLUTION, Bowker, New York, NY, 1974.

___H. Dippel, GERMANY AND THE AMERICAN REVOLUTION, University of NC Press, Chapel Hill, NC, 1977. [Sources in German Archives.]

___C. M. Andrews and F. G. Davenport, GUIDE TO THE MANUSCRIPT MATERIALS FOR THE HISTORY OF THE US IN BRITISH [ARCHIVES], Carnegie Institute, Washington, DC, 1908.

Warning

A good genealogical researcher is always on the lookout for the possibilities of errors and omissions in various original records and published materials. This is especially important with regard to indexes, since many of them are incomplete and sometimes contain erroneous entries. If at all possible, every bit of data should be double-checked and verifications in other sources should be earnestly sought.

Among the troublesome features of research, especially before 1900, are the spelling variations of surnames, given names, and geographic places. Quite often these items are spelled by the writer as he or she heard them. Thus you need to make every effort to imagine alternative spellings and to carefully seek them out in the indexes, records, and documents which you use.

Chapter 3

NATIONAL PUBLICATIONS

▄▄▄▄▄▄▄▄▄▄

1. Libraries

▄▄▄▄▄▄▄▄▄▄

In addition to original documents and microfilms of original documents, there are large numbers of published works (books) which contain lists of Revolutionary War soldiers and sailors and data on them. In this chapter, we will describe those which are national in scope, that is, those which carry lists and information on individuals from anywhere and everywhere in the colonies. You have already become acquainted with several of the most important ones of these in Chapter 2. In the next chapter (Chapter 4), we will describe published sources limited to individual states (colonies). In general, these published sources can be found in large genealogical libraries. You can consult them there for yourself, or you can write them, enclosing a long SASE, inquiring about the availability of the volumes you want, and asking for a list of researchers you can employ. Your local librarian can look up the detailed addresses for you in the current copy of

___American Library Association, AMERICAN LIBRARY DIREC-
TORY, Bowker Co., New York, NY, latest issue.

Among the larger genealogical libraries where you are likely to find many or even most of the volumes to be mentioned in this and the next chapter are the following:

___In AL: Birmingham Public Library, Library at Samford University in Birmingham, AL Archives and History Department in Montgomery, in AZ: Southern AZ Genealogical Society in Tucson, in AR: AR Genealogical Society in Little Rock, Little Rock Public Library, in CA: CA Genealogical Society in San Francisco, Los Angeles Public Library, San Diego Public Library, San Francisco Public Library, Sutro Library in San Francisco,

___In CO: Denver Public Library, in CT: CT State Library in Hartford, Godfrey Memorial Library in Middletown, in DC: Library of Congress in Washington, in FL: FL State Library in Tallahassee, Miami-Dade Public Library, Tampa Public Library, in GA: Atlanta Public Library, in ID: ID Genealogical Society, in IL: Newberry Library in Chicago, in IN: IN State Library in Indianapolis, Public Library of Fort Wayne, in IA: IA State Department of History and Archives in Des Moines,

___In KY: Filson Club Library in Louisville, KY Historical Society Library in Frankfort, in LA: LA State Library in Baton Rouge, in ME: ME State Library in Augusta, in MD: MD State Library in Annapolis, in

__MA__: Boston Public Library, New England Historic Genealogical Society Library in Boston, in __MI__: Detroit Public Library, in __MN__: Minneapolis Public Library, in __MS__: MS Department of Archives and History in Jackson, in __MO__: Kansas City Public Library, St. Louis Public Library,

In __NE__: NE State Historical Society in Lincoln, Omaha Public Library, in __NV__: Washoe County Library in Reno, in __NY__: NY Public Library, in __NC__: NC State Library in Raleigh, in __OH__: Cincinnati Public Library, OH State Library in Columbus, Western Reserve Historical Society in Cleveland, in __OK__: OK State Historical Society in Oklahoma City, in __OR__: Genealogical Forum of Portland, Portland Library Association, in __PA__: Historical Society of PA in Philadelphia, Carnegie Library of Pittsburgh,

In SC: The South Caroliniana Library in Columbia, in __SD__: State Historical Society in Pierre, in __TN__: TN State Library in Nashville, in __TX__: Dallas Public Library, Fort Worth Public Library, TX State Library in Austin, Houston Public Library, in __UT__: Brigham Young University Library in Provo, in __VA__: VA State Library, VA Historical Society Library in Richmond, in __WA__: Seattle Public Library, in __WV__: WV Department of Archives in Charleston, in __WI__: Milwaukee Public Library, State Historical Society in Madison.

There are two major libraries which deserve special mention. The first one is the Family History Library of the Genealogical Society of Utah, 50 East North Temple St., Salt Lake City, UT 84105. It is notable for three reasons: (1) It has an exceptionally extensive collection of Revolutionary War materials including almost everything mentioned in Chapters 2, 3, and 4. (2) It has put these materials on microfilm. (3) These microfilms may be borrowed through several hundred branches of the library (Family History Centers) which are located throughout the US. You can visit the main library and use the materials directly, or you can hire a researcher to do that, or you can go to a branch library (Family History Center) near you, locate what you want in their indexes, and have them order the films. When your films come, you will be notified. You can then return to the branch library and use their readers to examine your film. There may be several disadvantages to this branch library procedure. If there are quite a few films you want to read, your costs could mount up. Further, several weeks at a minimum are usually required for the films to come. And finally, you need to return to the library to examine the films, sometimes several times, since they will often not come together. Below is a list of cities having branch libraries. Their addresses and phone numbers may be found by looking under Church of Jesus Christ of Latter Day Saints in the local telephone directories. Be sure to call before you go to ascertain the hours they are open.

___In AL: Birmingham, Huntsville, in AK: Anchorage, Fairbanks, in AZ: Cottonwood, Flagstaff, Globe, Holbrook, Mesa, Page, Phoenix, Prescott, Safford, St. David, St. Johns, Show Low, Snowflake, Tucson, Winslow, Yuma, in AR: Little Rock,

___In CA: Anaheim, Bakersfield, Barstow, Blythe, Camarillo, Carlsbad, Cerritos, Chico, Covina, El Centro, Escondido, Eureka, Fairfield, Fresno, Garden Grove, Glendale, Gridley, Hacienda Heights, Hemet, La Crescenta, Lancaster, Long Beach, Los Angeles, Menlo Park, Modesto, Monterey, Napa, Newbury Park, Oakland, Orange, Palmdale, Palm Springs, Pasadena, Redding, Ridgecrest, Riverside, Sacramento, San Bernardino, San Diego, San Jose, San Luis Obispo, Santa Barbara, Santa Clara, Santa Maria, Santa Rosa, Simi Valley, Stockton, Upland, Ventura, Whittier,

___In CO: Arvada, Boulder, Colorado Springs, Cortez, Denver, Durango, Fort Collins, Glenwood Springs, Grand Junction, La Jara, Littleton, Montrose, Pueblo, in CT: Hartford, in DE: Newark, in FL: Boca Raton, Cocoa, Gainesville, Hialeah, Jacksonville, Lakeland, Marianna, Miami, Orlando, Pensacola, St. Petersburg, Tallahassee, Tampa, in GA: Dunwoody, Macon, Marietta, in HI: Hilo, Honolulu, Kaneohe, Kona, Laie,

___In ID: Blackfoot, Boise, Burley, Caldwell, Driggs, Firth, Idaho Falls, Iona, Lewiston, Malad, Montpelier, Moore, Nampa, Pocatello, Post Falls, Rexburg, Salmon, Shelley, Twin Falls, in IL: Champaign, Chicago Heights, Naperville, Rockford, Wilmette, in IN: Fort Wayne, Indianapolis, in IA: Cedar Rapids, Davenport, Des Moines, in KS: Topeka, Wichita, in KY: Hopkinsville, Lexington, Louisville, in LA: Baton Rouge, Shreveport,

___In ME: Augusta, in MD: Silver Spring, in MA: Boston, in MI: Bloomfield Hills, Grand Blanc, Grand Rapids, Lansing, Midland, Westland, in MN: Minneapolis, St. Paul, in MS: Hattiesburg, in MO: Columbia, Kansas City, Liberty, Springfield, St. Louis, in MT: Billings, Bozeman, Butte, Great Falls, Helena, Kalispell, Missoula, in NE: Omaha,

___In NV: Elko, Ely, Fallon, Las Vegas, Logandale, Reno, Sparks, in NH: Nashua, in NJ: East Brunswick, Morristown, in NM: Albuquerque, Farmington, Gallup, Grants, Las Cruces, Roswell, Santa Fe, in NY: Albany, Buffalo, Ithaca, New York, Plainview, Rochester, Syracuse, in NC: Asheville, Charlotte, Fayetteville, Hickory, Kinston, Raleigh, Wilmington, in OH: Cincinnati, Cleveland, Columbus, Dayton, Kirtland, Toledo,

___In OK: Norman, Oklahoma City, Tulsa, in OR: Beaverton, Bend, Coos
Bay, Corvallis, Eugene, Fairview, Grants Pass, Gresham, Klamath
Falls, LaGrande, Lake Oswego, Medford, Nyssa, Oregon City,
Portland, Prineville, Roseburg, Salem, The Dallas, in PA: Philadelphia,
Pittsburgh, Reading, State College, York, in SC: Charleston,
Columbia, Greenville, in TN: Chattanooga, Kingsport, Knoxville,
Memphis, Nashville, in TX: Austin, Beaumont, Corpus Christi, Dallas,
El Paso, Friendswood, Houston, Hurst, Longview, Lubbock, Odessa,
Richardson, San Antonio,
___In UT: Beaver, Blanding, Bountiful, Brigham City, Cedar City, Delta,
Duchesne, Fillmore, Heber City, Hurricane, Kanab, Lehi, Logan,
Moroni, Mt. Pleasant, Nephi, Ogden, Parowan, Price, Provo, Richfield,
Riverton, Roosevelt, St. George, Sandy, Santaquin, Springville,
Trementon, Vernal, in VA: Annandale, Charlottesville, Fairfax,
Norfolk, Oakton, Richmond, Roanoke,
___In WA: Bellevue, Bellingham, Bremerton, Everett, Longview, Moses
Lake, Mt. Vernon, Olympia, Pasco, Pullman, Quincy, Richland,
Seattle, Spokane, Sumner, Tacoma, Vancouver, Walla Walla,
Wenatchee, Yakima, in WI: Appleton, Beloit, Milwaukee, in WY:
Afton, Casper, Cheyenne, Cody, Evanston, Gillette, Green River,
Kemmerer, Lovell, Rock Springs, Worland.
The Family History Library is constantly adding new branches so this list
will probably be out-of-date by the time you read it. An SASE and a $2
fee to them (address in first paragraph above) will bring you an up-to-date
listing of Family History Centers.

The second major library which deserves special mention is the
Genealogical Library of the National Society of Daughters of the
American Revolution, 1776 D St., NW, Washington, DC 20008. For many
years this society has been exceptionally active in tracing Revolutionary
War participants and in establishing lineages down to the present. They
have published an amazing volume of material, much of which is referenced in this book. Their national library contains a very large collection
of Revolutionary War materials including most of those mentioned in this
volume. The library exists primarily to serve their large membership, and
therefore they cannot do research for others. However, they do make
their library available to non-members (or researchers non-members
employ) for a small daily fee, except during parts of April and May.

---

2. Roster, rolls and lists

Two major military service lists were
indicated in section 2 of Chapter 2, as well
as two major claims volumes. The two

major lists, as you will recall, were the DAR PATRIOT INDEX [over 140,000 names], and Rider's AMERICAN GENEALOGICAL-BIOGRAPHICAL INDEX [incomplete, but well over 100,000 names]. The purpose of this section is to point out to you a number of other publications which carry lists of Revolutionary War participants. The lists given in this section are largely lists based on military service. Lists based on pensions, bounty land claims, and other types of claims will be given in sections to follow.

Included among the volumes which can be used for both soldiers and their commissioned officers are:

___C. E. Chunn, NOT BY BREAD ALONE, Society of the Descendants of Washingtons Army at Valley Forge, Valley Forge, PA, 1981. Those who served at Valley Forge.

___W. Coburn, THE BATTLE OF APRIL 19, 1775 IN LEXINGTON, CONCORD, ETC., Lexington Historical Society, Lexington, MA, 1922. [About 3600 men.]

___G. R. Crowther, SURNAME INDEX TO 65 VOLUMES OF COLONIAL AND REVOLUTIONARY PEDIGREES, National Genealogical Society, Publication No. 27, Washington, DC, 1964.

___T. N. Dupuy and G. M. Hammerman, PEOPLE AND EVENTS OF THE AMERICAN REVOLUTION, Bowker, New York, NY, 1974. [About 1400 biographical profiles.]

___W. H. English, CONQUEST OF THE COUNTRY NORTHWEST OF THE RIVER OHIO, 1778-83, Bowen-Merrill, Indianapolis, IN, 1896, 2 volumes. Soldiers in Clarks troops.

___P. Force, AMERICAN ARCHIVES, 4th Series (6 volumes), 5th Series (2 volumes), Washington, DC, 1837-53.

___C. E. Godfrey, THE COMMANDER-IN-CHIEFS GUARD, REVOLUTIONARY WAR, Clearfield Co., Baltimore, MD, 1995. [Over 350 soldiers.]

___M. H. Harding, GEORGE ROGERS CLARK AND HIS MEN, MILITARY RECORDS, KY Historical Society, Frankfort, KY, 1981.

___P. L. Hatcher, GRAVES OF REVOLUTIONARY PATRIOTS, Pioneer Heritage Press, Dallas, TX, 1987, 4 volumes. [Over+58,000 entries.]

___B. J. Lossing, THE PICTORIAL FIELD BOOK OF THE REVOLU-TION, Polyanthos, New Orleans, LA, 1973. [Thousands of names.]

___National DAR, REPORTS (issued annually), The Society, Washington, DC, 1899-, volume 1-. [Revolutionary War biographies, muster rolls, lists, over 54,000 burials, indexed in each issue.]

___National DAR, INDEX TO THE ROLLS OF HONOR (ANCESTOR'S INDEX) IN THE LINEAGE BOOKS, VOLUME 1-160, Genealogical Publishing Co., Baltimore, MD, 1972, 2 volumes. [Over 50,000 names.]

___National DAR, DAR MAGAZINE, The Society, Washington, DC, 1897-, volume 1-, to be used with GENEALOGICAL GUIDE: MASTER INDEX OF GENEALOGY IN THE DAR MAGAZINE (VOLUMES 1-84), DAR of MO, Kansas City, MO, 1951, and SUPPLEMENTS TO THE GENEALOGICAL GUIDE, various DAR Chapters, Supplement 1 (volumes 85-89), Supplement 2 (volumes 91-101), Supplement 3 (volumes 100-104), 1956, 1971, 1974.

___NY Historical Society, MUSTER AND PAY ROLLS OF THE WAR OF THE REVOLUTION, Collections of the NY Historical Society, Series 47-48, New York, NY, 1914-6. [Continental regiments and lines, militia, troops from Canada, CT, MD, MA, NH, NJ, NY, NC, PA, RI, SC, VA.]

___C. S. Peterson, KNOWN MILITARY DEAD DURING THE AMERICAN REVOLUTIONARY WAR, Genealogical Publishing Co., Baltimore, MD, 1967. [Over 10,000 names.]

___W. T. R. Saffell, RECORDS OF THE REVOLUTIONARY WAR, Saffell, New York, NY, 1858. Officers, soldiers, prisoners.

___Sons of the American Revolution, A NATIONAL REGISTER OF THE SOCIETY OF THE SONS OF THE AMERICAN REVOLUTION, Kellogg, New York, NY, 1902.

Further lists can be located by using:

___L. Horowitz, A BIBLIOGRAPHY OF MILITARY NAME LISTS FROM PRE-1675 TO 1900: A GUIDE TO GENEALOGICAL SOURCES, Scarecrow Press, Metuchen, NJ, 1990, pages 70-451.

For officers of the army, the following volumes will be helpful. Some of these books are doubly valuable in that they also give the military units in which the officers served, and therefore they provide you with the organizational pattern of the army.

___T. H. S. Hamersly, COMPLETE REGULAR ARMY REGISTER OF THE US, 1778-1879, The Author, New York, NY, 1880. [About 2500 officers with rank and organization.]

___F. B. Heitman, HISTORICAL REGISTER OF OFFICERS OF THE CONTINENTAL ARMY, Genealogical Publishing Co., Baltimore, MD, 1969. [About 15,000 officers.]

___B. Metcalf, ORIGINAL MEMBERS AND OTHER OFFICERS ELIGIBLE TO THE SOCIETY OF CINCINNATI, 1783-1938, Shenandoah Publishing House, Strasburg, VA, 1938. [Over 3000 officers.]

___W. H. Powell, LIST OF OFFICERS OF THE ARMY OF THE US, 1779-1900, Hamersly, New York, NY, 1900. [About 1000 officers and their organizations.]

There are also some volumes relating particularly to the navy and the marines. Should your ancestor have served in either of these branches of the service, the following books should be consulted:

___G. W. Allen, A NAVAL HISTORY OF THE AMERICAN REVOLUTION, Houghton Mifflin, New York, NY, 1913. [Ships and names of officers.]

___E. W. Callahan, LIST OF OFFICERS OF THE NAVY OF THE US AND OF MARINE CORPS, 1775-1900, Hamersly, New York, NY, 1901.

___T. H. S. Hamersly, COMPLETE NAVY REGISTER OF THE US, 1776-1887, The Author, New York, NY, 1888. [Names of naval officers.]

___M. and J. Kaminkow, MARINERS OF THE AMERICAN REVOLU-TION, Magna Carta Book Co., Baltimore, MD, 1967. [Almost 3000 men.]

___E. N. McClellan, MARINE OFFICERS OF THE REVOLUTION, DAR Magazine, volume 66, 1932, pp. 560-8.

___O. E. Monnette, SPIRIT OF PATRIOTISM, Standard Print Co., Los Angeles, CA, 1917. Naval personnel.

___C. R. Smith, MARINES IN THE REVOLUTION, History and Museums Division, US Marine Corps, Washington, DC, 1975. [About 120 marine officer biographies.]

___US Naval History Division, NAVAL DOCUMENTS OF THE AMERICAN REVOLUTION, Government Printing Office, Washington, DC, 1964, volumes 1, 4, 5.

___M. E. Witt, AN ALPHABETICAL LIST OF NAVY, MARINE, AND PRIVATEER PERSONNEL, Mew Publishing, Dallas, TX, 1986.

The book by Allen can be especially useful because of its ship listings.

3. Pensions and pensioners

The pensions given to Revolutionary War veterans are the most fruitful source of information on individuals. They often provide a great deal of information not only on the veteran, but also on his family and on their movements. During the war and shortly thereafter, pension legislation was passed. These laws provided for benefits to be paid to disabled veterans and to widows and orphans of those that were killed or those that died as a result of their service. In 1818, the US

Congress broadened the benefits by providing pensions for all who had served in the Continental Army for nine months or until the end of the war and who were in need of financial help. In 1820 pensioners were required to prove their financial need, and as a result, quite a few were taken off the rolls. A law in 1823 restored many. In 1828, further broadening of pension coverage was carried out in that full pay for life was voted for officers who had previously been granted half pay and for enlisted men who had received a one-year pay bonus on being discharged.

In 1832, legislation was passed providing pensions for all servicemen, both Continental Army and militia, who had been on active duty for at least six months. Then, in 1836, pensions were granted to widows who had been married before the end of their husband's war service. The regulations were gradually eased until by 1856 any widow of a soldier or any soldier serving two weeks or in a battle could receive a pension. Unfortunately, most pension applications received by the Secretary of War before 08 November 1800 were destroyed in a fire on that date or in the fire when the British burned Washington in 1814. Some few have survived and they have been filed in the National Archives pension and bounty land application files.

In section 2 of Chapter 2, you have already been acquainted with the largest of the pension application listings, namely the INDEX OF REVOLUTIONARY WAR PENSION APPLICATIONS IN THE NATIONAL ARCHIVES. [About 80,000 names.] There are several other pension-related volumes which may provide you with information:

___M. J. Clark, THE PENSION LISTS OF 1792-95, Genealogical Publishing Co., Baltimore, MD, 1991.

___US War Department, REVOLUTIONARY PENSIONERS OF 1813, Genealogical Publishing Co., Baltimore, MD, 1959.

___US War Department, A REPORT OF THE NAMES, RANK, AND LINE OF EVERY PERSON PLACED ON THE PENSION LIST AS OF THE ACT OF 18TH MARCH, 1818, Genealogical Publishing Co., Baltimore, MD, 1955. [Over 16,000 names.]

___US War Department, REVOLUTIONARY PENSIONERS OF 1818, Genealogical Publishing Co., Baltimore, MD, 1959. [Over 5800 listings.]

___M. J. Clark, THE PENSION LIST OF 1820, Genealogical Publishing Co., Baltimore, MD, 1991.

___M. J. Clark, INDEX TO THE US INVALID PENSION RECORDS, Genealogical Publishing Co., Baltimore, MD, 1991.

___US War Department, THE PENSION ROLL OF 1835, Genealogical Publishing Co., Baltimore, MD, 1968, 4 volumes.

___US War Department, PENSIONERS OF REVOLUTIONARY WAR STRUCK OFF THE ROLL, 1836, Genealogical Publishing Co., Baltimore, MD, 1969. [6000 names.]

___US Department of State, A CENSUS OF PENSIONERS FOR REVOLUTIONARY SERVICE TAKEN IN 1840, Genealogical Publishing Co., Baltimore, MD, 1974. [More than 25,000 names.] To be used with Genealogical Society, Church of Jesus Christ of LDS, A GENERAL INDEX TO A CENSUS OF PENSIONERS FOR REVOLUTIONARY SERVICE, Genealogical Publishing Co., Baltimore, MD, 1965.

___US Department of the Interior, REJECTED OR SUSPENDED APPLICATIONS FOR REVOLUTIONARY WAR PENSIONS, 32nd Congress, First Session, Senate Executive Document 37, Genealogical Publishing Co., Baltimore, MD, 1969, 1974. [11,000 listings and index in the 1974 reprint.]

___AMERICAN STATE PAPERS, CLAIMS, Gales and Seaton, Washington, DC, 1834.

___ABSTRACTS OF REVOLUTIONARY WAR PENSION ABSTRACTS, National Genealogical Society Quarterly, volumes 17-41, 1929-52.

---

4. Bounty land and other claims

In section 2 of Chapter 2, you have seen the major reference works to federal bounty land claims and other claims. The volume indexing bounty land claims was the INDEX OF REVOLUTIONARY WAR PENSION APPLICATIONS IN THE NATIONAL ARCHIVES [about 80,000 names], even though the title does not indicate it. The most important book indexing late pay certificates was the REGISTER OF CERTIFICATES ISSUED BY JOHN PIERCE TO OFFICERS AND SOLDIERS OF THE CONTINENTAL ARMY [over 93,000 entries].

Additional claims volumes and microfilms which can provide further listings are as follows:

___W. Lowrie and W. S. Franklin, AMERICAN STATE PAPERS, 1789-1823, CLAIMS VOLUME, US Congress, Washington, DC, 1834.

___National Archives, PAPERS OF THE CONTINENTAL CONGRESS, 1774-89, The Archives, Washington, DC, Microfilm Publication M247, 204 rolls, to be used with INDEX.

___National Archives, US REVOLUTIONARY WAR BOUNTY LAND WARRANTS USED IN THE US MILITARY DISTRICT OF OH, The Archives, Washington, DC, Microfilm Publication M829, 16 rolls.

___C. N. Smith, FEDERAL LAND SERIES: LAND PATENTS ISSUED BY THE US GOVERNMENT, American Library Association, Chicago, IL, 1972-86, 5 volumes.

___US House of Representatives, DIGESTED SUMMARY AND ALPHABETICAL LIST OF PRIVATE CLAIMS, 32nd Congress, 1st Session, House Miscellaneous Document, Genealogical Publishing Co., Baltimore, MD, 1970, 3 volumes. [60,000 listings.]

___US Congress, LIST OF NAMES OF SUCH OFFICERS AND SOLDIERS OF THE REVOLUTIONARY ARMY AS HAVE ACQUIRED A RIGHT TO LANDS AND WHO HAVE NOT YET APPLIED THEREFOR, 20th Congress, 1st Session, Senate Document 42, 1828. [About 2800 names.]

In addition to federal bounty land, many of the states also offered bounty land to their veterans (GA, MD, MA, NY, NC, PA, SC, VA). The states of GA, MD, NY, PA, and SC granted bounty land within their own borders. MA gave land in ME, NC gave land in TN, and VA gave land in both KY and OH. Many of these grants are listed in:

___L. D. Bockstruck, REVOLUTIONARY WAR BOUNTY LAND GRANTS AWARDED BY STATE GOVERNMENTS, Genealogical Publishing Co., Baltimore, MD, 1996. [About 36,000 names.]

The states of CT, DE, NH, NJ, and RI did not grant bounty lands, but CT did award land to those whose property was destroyed by the British. Records on state bounty lands may be located in state archives (see section 4, Chapter 2), and state publications relating to them will be listed in Chapter 4.

5. Other patriot lists

In addition to general listings of Americans in the Revolutionary War, there are also numerous compilations of lists relating to special groups, some of these groups being American patriots, others of them being groups who sided with the British. Notable among the patriot listings are those having to do with prisoners, the Irish, the Jewish, women, chaplains, blacks, medical men, and the French. The major groups siding with the British were the American Loyalists and the German mercenaries who were hired by the British.

American prisoners were discussed and/or listed in several volumes, the following being among the most useful ones:

___AMERICAN PRISONERS IN MILL PRISON AT PLYMOUTH, ENGLAND IN 1782, SC Historical and Genealogical Magazine, volume 10, 1909, pp. 116-24.

___L. G. Bowman, CAPTIVE AMERICANS: PRISONERS DURING THE AMERICAN REVOLUTION, Ohio University Press, Athens, OH, 1978.

___D. B. Dandridge, AMERICAN PRISONERS OF THE REVOLUTION, Genealogical Publishing Co., Baltimore, MD, 1967. [Same 8000 as previous reference.]

___M. and J. Kaminkow, MARINERS OF THE AMERICAN REVOLU-TION, Magna Carta, Baltimore, MD, 1967. [About 2500 who were captured.]

___C. McHenry, REBEL PRISONERS AT QUEBEC, 1778-83, The Author, Lawrenceburg, IN, 1981.

___W. T. R. Saffell, RECORDS OF THE REVOLUTIONARY WAR, Genealogical Publishing Co., Baltimore, MD, 1969.

___Society of Old Brooklynites, A CHRISTMAS REMINDER, BEING THE NAMES OF ABOUT 8000 PERSONS CONFINED ON BOARD BRITISH PRISON SHIPS, The Society, Brooklyn, NY, 1888. [About 8000.]

The dedicated participation of Irish patriots, their special contributions, and some listings are provided in a number of books. Among them are the following:

___J. Haltigan, THE IRISH IN THE AMERICAN REVOLUTION, The Author, Washington, DC, 1907.

___T. H. Maginnis, THE IRISH CONTRIBUTION TO AMERICA'S INDEPENDENCE, Doire, Philadelphia, PA, 1913. [About 1000 names.]

___C. Murphy, THE IRISH IN THE AMERICAN REVOLUTION, Murphy Publ., Groveland, MA, 1975.

___M. J. O'Brien, A HIDDEN PHASE OF AMERICA'S HISTORY: IRELAND'S PART IN AMERICA'S STRUGGLE FOR LIBERTY, Dodd, Mead, New York, NY, 1919. [About 5000 names.]

Two helpful volumes describing the important contributions made by Jews in the War for American Independence are:

___S. G. Gumpertz, JEWISH LEGION OF VALOR: THE STORY OF JEWISH HEROES IN THE WARS OF THE REPUBLIC, New York, NY, 1934.

___S. Wolf, THE AMERICAN JEW AS PATRIOT, SOLDIER, AND CITIZEN, Levytype Co, Philadelphia, PA, 1895.

Should you care to consider the important roles which were played by some outstanding <u>women</u> of the Revolutionary Era, the following works will serve you very well:

___C. E. Claghorn, WOMEN PATRIOTS OF THE AMERICAN REVOLUTION, Scarecrow Press, Metuchen, NJ, 1991.

___E. F. Ellet, THE WOMEN OF THE AMERICAN REVOLUTION, Haskell, New York, NY, 1969. [Over 160 biographies.]

___P. Engle, WOMEN IN THE AMERICAN REVOLUTION, Follett, Chicago, IL, 1976. [18 biographies.]

___E. Evans, WEATHERING THE STORM, Scribner's Sons, New York, NY, 1975. [11 diaries.]

Chaplains and other <u>clergy</u> were quite active during the War. Special attention is paid to them in these notable volumes:

___A. H. Germain, CATHOLIC MILITARY AND NAVAL CHAPLAINS, 1776-1917, Washington, DC, 1929.

___E. M. Hayward, THE CHAPLAINS AND CLERGY OF THE REVOLUTION, A LIST COMPILED FROM BAPTIST PERIODICALS AT FRANKLIN COLLEGE, Ridgewood, NJ, 1947.

___J. T. Headley, THE CHAPLAINS AND CLERGY OF THE REVOLUTION, Scribner's Sons, New York, NY, 1864.

___C. R. McLane, AMERICAN CHAPLAINS OF THE REVOLUTION, National Society of the Sons of the American Revolution, Louisville, KY, 1991.

___E. F. Williams, SOLDIERS OF GOD: THE CHAPLAINS OF THE REVOLUTIONARY WAR, Carlton Press, New York, NY, 1975. [Over 200 men.]

Some worthwhile beginnings in studying <u>blacks</u> who fought for independence have been made. Their contribution was quite important, as the books below will attest. Several of these contain sizable listings of names.

___B. Davis, BLACK HEROES OF THE AMERICAN REVOLUTION, Harcourt Brace Jovanovich, New York, NY, 1976.

___P. S. Foner, BLACKS IN THE AMERICAN REVOLUTION, Greenwood, Westport, CT, 1976.

___R. E. Greene, BLACK COURAGE, 1775-83, National Society DAR, Washington, DC, 1984.

___National Archives, INSPECTION ROLLS OF SLAVES WHO LEFT NY CITY WITH THE BRITISH IN 1783, The Archives, Washington, DC, Microfilm M247, roll 66, and Microfilm M332, roll 7.

___W. C. Nell, THE COLORED PATRIOTS OF THE AMERICAN
REVOLUTION, Arno Press, New York, NY, 1968.

___D. L. Newman, LIST OF BLACK SERVICEMEN COMPILED
FROM THE WAR DEPARTMENT COLLECTION OF
REVOLUTIONARY WAR RECORDS, National Archives Special
List Number 36, Washington, DC, 1984. [About 1100 names.]

___M. Stewart, BLACK SOLDIERS IN THE AMERICAN
REVOLUTIONARY WAR, University Press, Centre, AL, 1978.

___E. G. Wilson, THE LOYAL BLACKS, Capricorn, New York, NY,
1976.

Another topic that has been of great interest is that of the practice of
medicine during the American Revolution. A couple of worthwhile works
treat the medical practitioners of the time:

___L. C. Duncan, MEDICAL MEN IN THE AMERICAN
REVOLUTION, Army Military History Institute, Carlisle Barracks,
PA, 1931.

___J. M. Toner, THE MEDICAL MEN OF THE REVOLUTION, Col-
lins, Philadelphia, PA, 1876.

There are also some specialized volumes dealing with Scots and Polish
in the War.

___J. P. MacLean, AN HISTORICAL ACCOUNT OF THE
SETTLEMENT OF SCOTCH HIGHLANDERS IN AMERICA
PRIOR TO 1783, Genealogical Publishing Co., Baltimore, MD 1968.
[Scottish regiments, lists, and biographical sketches.]

___M. Haiman, POLAND AND THE AMERICAN REVOLUTIONARY
WAR, Polish Roman Catholic Union of America, Chicago, IL, 1932.

___J. A. Wytreal, POLES IN AMERICAN HISTORY AND
TRADITION, Endurance Press, Detroit, MI, 1969.

Finally, as you have already seen in the first chapter, the French
played a very important part in the conflict. Early in the War, they
supported the rebelling colonies with supplies, and several Frenchmen
entered the Continental Army as leaders. Then, after Saratoga, the
French entered the War in full force, sending large numbers of both navy
and army personnel into the American arena. Some of these Frenchmen
remained here. Volumes listing participants and describing their activities
include:

___T. Balch, THE FRENCH IN AMERICA DURING THE WAR OF
INDEPENDENCE, 1777-83, Porter and Coates, Philadelphia, PA,
1891-5, 2 volumes. [About 1000 officers.]

___G. Bodinier, DICTIONNAIRE DES OFFICERS DE L'ARMEE ROYALE QUI ONT COMBATTU AUX ETATS-UNIS PENDANT LA GUERRE D'INDEPENDENCE, 1776-83, Ministere de la Defense, Vincennes, France, 1983.

___L. G. M. Du Bessey de Contention, LA SOCIETE DES CINCINNATI DE FRANCE ET LA GUERRE D'AMERIQUE, Picard, Paris, France, 1934. Officers.

___A. B. Gardiner, THE SOCIETY OF THE CINCINNATI IN FRANCE, FRENCH MEMBERS FROM THE WAR OF REVOLUTION, RI State Society of the Cincinnati, Providence, RI, 1905.

___L. B. Kennett, THE FRENCH FORCES IN AMERICA, 1780-3, Greenwood, Westport, CT, 1977.

___A. Lasseray, LES FRANCAIS SOUS LE TREIZE ETOILES (1776-83) CINQ PLANCHES HORS TEXTE, Protat Freres, Macon, France, 1935.

___Ministere des Affaires Etrangeres, France, LES COMBATTANTS FRANCAIS DE LA GUERRE AMERICAINE, Genealogical Publishing Co., Baltimore, MD, 1903-5, 1969. [About 45,000 names.]

___J. Merlant, SOLDIERS AND SAILORS OF FRANCE IN THE AMERICAN WAR FOR INDEPENDENCE, Scribner's Sons, New York, NY, 1920.

___V. de Noailles, MARINS ET SOLDATS FRANCAIS EN AMERIQUE PENDANT LA GUERRE DE L'INDEPENDENCE, Perrin et Cie, Paris, France, 1903.

In the next section, records relating to those loyal to the British cause will be discussed.

6. Loyalists and Germans

During the Revolutionary War there were many colonists who chose to side with the British and therefore to oppose the rebellion. As the events preceding the War led into actual combat, more and more British sympathizers left the colonies for Canada, Florida, England, and the West Indies. Quite a few simply moved into the wilderness beyond the western frontiers. Others chose to remain and to maintain a low profile. Others enlisted in the British regular army or navy, an estimated 50,000 fighting either as British regular army members or as Loyalist militia. About 15,000 Loyalist militiamen organized themselves and chose their own officers during the British occupations of GA, NC, SC, NY, and ME. Those in the southern colonies saw the most intense military action. In other areas, Loyalist guerrillas launched raids and skirmishes against the patriots, but made little major impact for the British. In areas where the rebels dominated, persecution of Loyalists began before the war and continued throughout it. In many places Loyalists were harassed, expelled, and/or their property confiscated. The total number of Loyalists leaving America was about 100,000. Some of these Loyalists eventually returned to the US, and some switched sides during the war. Listings of troops, names of those filing claims with Great Britain for war losses, and names of those settling outside the rebelling colonies are included in these volumes:

___W. Bruce Antliff, LOYALIST SETTLEMENTS 1783-1789, NEW EVIDENCE OF CANADIAN LOYALIST CLAIMS, Ontario Govt. Bookstore, Toronto, ONT, 1985.

___British Exchequer and Audit Department, AMERICAN LOYALIST CLAIMS, Series 1, Nendeln, Liechtenstein, 1972, 30 rolls microfilm.

___W. Brown, THE GOOD AMERICANS: THE LOYALISTS IN THE AMERICAN REVOLUTION, Morrow and Co., New York, NY, 1969.

___P. J. Bunnell, THE NEW LOYALIST INDEX, Heritage Books, Bowie, MD, 1989. [5000 Loyalists].

___THE CENTENNIAL OF THE SETTLEMENT OF UPPER CANADA BY THE UNITED EMPIRE LOYALISTS, 1784-1984, Rose Publishing Co., Toronto, ONT, 1885.

___M. J. Clark, LOYALISTS IN THE SOUTHERN CAMPAIGN OF THE REVOLUTIONARY WAR, Genealogical Publishing Co., Baltimore, MD, 1980, volume 1 [About 15,000 Loyalists of FL, GA, LA, MS, NC, and SC], volume 2 [About 10,000 Loyalists of MD, PA, and VA], volume 3 [About 10,000 Loyalists of NY, NJ, and other colonies].

___D. P. Coke, THE ROYAL COMMISSION ON THE LOSSES AND SERVICES OF AMERICAN LOYALISTS, 1783-5, Arno Press, New York, NY, 1969. [About 500 claimants].

___P. W. Coldham, AMERICAN LOYALIST CLAIMS, National Genealogical Society, Washington, DC, 1980, volume 1. [About 2700 names].

___L. Corupe, INDEX TO THE LOYALISTS OF THE EASTERN TOWNSHIPS OF QUEBEC, The Author, Quebec, CAN, 1984.

___N. K. Crowder, EARLY ONTARIO STTLERS, A SOURCE BOOK, Genealogical Publishing Co, Baltimore, MD, 1993.

___S. Dubeau, NEW BRUNSWICK LOYALISTS, Generation Press, Agincourt, Ontario, 1983.

___C. S. Dwyer, INDEX TO AMERICAN LOYALISTS CLAIMS, Series I and II, The Author, DeFuniak Springs, FL, 1985-86, 2 volumes.

___J. Eardley-Wilmot, HISTORICAL VIEW OF AMERICAN LOYAL-ISTS AT THE CLOSE OF THE WAR WITH AN ACCOUNT OF COMPENSATION GRANTED TO THEM BY PARLIAMENT, Gregg, Boston, MA, 1972.

___H. E. Edgerton, THE ROYAL COMMISSION ON THE LOSSES AND SERVICES OF AMERICAN LOYALISTS, 1783-85, Roxburghe Club, Oxford, ENG, 1915.

___E. K. Fitzgerald, LOYALIST LISTS, Ontario Genealogical Soicety, Ontario, 1984. [Over 2000 names.]

___E. K. Fitzgerald, ONTARIO PEOPLE, 1796-1803, Genealogical Publishing Co., Baltimore, MD, 1993.

___A. Frazer, UNITED EMPIRE LOYALISTS INQUIRY OF EVIDENCE IN CANADIAN CLAIMS, King's Printer, Toronto, Ontario, 1905.

___M. B. Fryer and W. A. Smy, ROLLS OF THE PROVINCIAL LOYALIST CORPS, CANADIAN COMMAND, AMERICAN REVOLUTIONARY PERIOD, Dundurn Press, Toronto, CAN, 1981.

___M. Gilroy, LOYALISTS AND LAND SETTLEMENT IN NOVA SCOTIA, Clearfield Co., Baltimore, MD, 1995. [10,000 Loyalists.]

___J. Hall, BRITISH, GERMAN, AND LOYALIST OFFICERS IN THE AMERICAN REVOLUTION, The Author, Magna, UT, 1990.

___I. L. Hill, SOME LOYALISTS AND OTHERS, The Author, Frederictown, NB, 1977.

___P. R. N. Katcher, ENCYCLOPEDIA OF BRITISH, PROVINCIAL, AND GERMAN ARMY UNITS, 1775-83, Stackpole, Harrisburg, PA, 1973.

___Library of Congress, CLAIMS FILED WITH THE ROYAL COM-MISSION ON LOSSES AND SERVICES OF AMERICAN LOYALISTS, Microfilm Copies of Audit Office 12 and 13 Documents, Public Record Office, London, England.

___M. R. Livingston, UPPER CANADA SONS AND DAUGHTERS OF THE UNITED EMPIRE LOYALISTS, Brown and Martin, Kingston, Ontario, CAN, 1981.

___M. B. Norton, THE BRITISH-AMERICAN: THE LOYALIST EXILES IN ENGLAND, 1774-89, Constable, London, ENG, 1974.

___THE OLD UNITED EMPIRE LOYALIST LISTS, Genealogical Publishing Co., Baltimore, MD, 1976.

___G. Palmer, BIOGRAPHICAL SKETCHES OF LOYALISTS OF THE AMERICAN REVOLUTION, Meckler Publ., Westport, CT, 1984.

___T. P. Peters, THE AMERICAN LOYALIST AND THE PLANTATION PERIOD IN THE BAHAMA ISLANDS, microfilm, GA State Archives, Atlanta, GA.

___G. B. Pipes, LOYALISTS ALL, New Brunswick United Empire Loyalist Association, St. John, New Brunswick, 1985.

___W. D. Reid, THE LOYALISTS IN ONTARIO, Hunterdon House, Lambertville, NJ, 1973. [Over 9000 names].

___A. E. Ryerson, LOYALISTS OF AMERICA, THEIR TIMES FROM 1620 TO 1816, Briggs, Toronto, CAN, 1880.

___L. Sabine, BIOGRAPHICAL SKETCHES OF LOYALISTS OF THE AMERICAN REVOLUTION, Kennikat, Port Washington, NY, 1966.

___L. H. Smith, Jr., NOVA SCOTIA IMMIGRANTS TO 1867, Genealogical Publishing Co, Baltimore, MD, 1992.

___J. J. Talman, LOYALIST NARRATIVES FROM UPPER CANADA, Greenwood Press, New York, NY, 1969.

___Toronto Branch, United Empire Loyalists Association, LOYALIST LINEAGES OF CANADA, The Branch, Toronto, Ontario, Canada, 1985.

___United Empire Loyalists, ENQUIRY INTO THE LOSSES AND SERVICES IN CONSEQUENCE OF THEIR LOYALTY: EVIDENCE IN THE CANADIAN CLAIMS, L. K. Cameron, Toronto, CAN, 1905.

___E. C. Wright, THE LOYALISTS OF NEW BRUNSWICK, Fredericktown, New Brunswick, 1955.

More information on Loyalist records may be obtained from The United Empire Loyalist Association of Canada, 23 Prince Arthur Ave., Toronto, Ontario M52 LB2. Useful guides to other sources of Loyalist records include:

___R. S. Allen, LOYALIST LITERATURE, AN ANNOTATED BIBLIOGRAPHIC GUIDE, Dundurn Press, Toronto, Ontario, 1982.

___P. J. Bunnell, RESEARCH GUIDE TO LOYALIST ANCESTORS, Heritage Books, Bowie, MD, 1990.

___H. Leventhal and J. E. Mooney, A BIBLIOGRAPHY OF LOYAL-ISTS MATERIALS IN THE US, Proceedings of the American Antiquarian Society, Volumes 82, 85-90, 1973, 1976-80.

___G. Palmer, A BIBLIOGRAPHY OF LOYALIST SOURCE MATERIAL IN THE US, CANADA, AND GREAT BRITAIN, Meckler Publ., Westport, CT, 1982.

___J. Peterson, THE LOYALIST GUIDE: NOVA SCOTIAN LOYALISTS AND THEIR DOCUMENTS, NS Public Archives, Halifax, NS, 1983.

Almost 34,000 German mercenaries fought with the British during the Revolutionary War. They participated in every major campaign. It is estimated that about 6300 of them died of disease, 1200 were killed in battle, and that about 7000 deserted to remain here in this country or to go to Canada. Others received permission after the War was ended to stay here. Although the Germans were all loosely termed Hessians, probably because their early commanders-in-chief were from Hesse, they came from several different areas in Germany. About 19,000 were from Hesse-Kassel, about 5700 from Braunschweig, about 2400 from Hesse-Hanau, about 2400 from Ansbach-Bayreuth, about 1200 from Waldeck, and about 1200 from Anhalt-Zerbst. About 10,500 of those from Hesse-Kassel returned, 2700 from Braunschweig, 1400 from Hesse-Hanau, 1200 from Ansbach-Bayreuth, 500 from Waldeck, and 1000 from Anhalt-Zerbst. The following works may be consulted in order to try to find an ancestor whom you believe originally came here as a German soldier:

___R. Atwood, THE HESSIANS: MERCENARIES FROM HESSEN-KASSEL IN THE AMERICAN REVOLUTION, Cambridge, New York, NY, 1980. [Officers.]

___I. Auerbach and O. Froelich, HESSISCHE TRUPPEN IN AMERICANISCHEN UNABHANGIGKEITSKRIEG(HETRINA), St. Louis Genealogical Society, St. Louis, MO, 1972 ff, 5 volumes. [Index of Hessian troops.]

___B. E. Burgoyne, WALDECK SOLDIERS OF THE AMERICAN REVOLUTION, Heritage Books, Bowie, MD, 1991.

___V. E. DeMarce, AN ANNOTATED LIST OF 317 FORMER GERMAN SOLDIERS WHO CHOSE TO REMAIN IN CANADA AFTER THE AMERICAN REVOLUTION, The Author, Arlington, VA, 1981.

___V. E. DeMarce, MERCENARY TROOOPS FROM ANHALT-ZERBST, GERMANY, WHO SERVED WITH THE BRITISH FORCES DURING THE AMERICAN REVOLUTION, Westland Publications, McNeal, AZ, 1984, 2 volumes.

___V. E. DeMarce, THE SETTLEMENT OF FORMER GERMAN AUXILLIARY TROOPS IN CANADA AFTER THE AMERICAN REVOLUTION, The Author, Arlington, VA, 1982, with SUPPLEMENT, Reisinger, Sparta, WI, 1984.

___M. P. Dickore, HESSIANS SOLDIERS IN THE AMERICAN REVOLUTION: RECORDS OF MARRIAGES AND BAPTISMS IN AMERICA FOR TWO REGIMENTS, 1776-82, Krehbiel Co., Cincinnati, OH, 1959.

___M. von Eelking, THE GERMAN ALLIED TROOPS IN THE NORTH AMERICAN WAR OF INDEPENDENCE, 1776-83, Genealogical Publishing Co., Baltimore, MD, 1893. [About 1000 officers.]

___A. F. Geisler, GESCHICHTE UND ZUSTAND, Dessau und Leipzig, 1784. [German officers.]

___C. W. Heckert, THE GERMAN-AMERICAN DIARY, McClin Printing Co., Parsons, WV, 1980. [Lists of German soldiers.]

___P. R. N. Katcher, ENCYCLOPEDIA OF BRITISH, PROVINCIAL, AND GERMAN ARMY UNITS, 1775-83, Stackpole, Harrisburg, PA, 1973.

___E. J. Lowell, THE HESSIANS AND OTHER GERMAN AUXILIARIES OF GREAT BRITAIN IN THE REVOLUTIONARY WAR, Corner House, Williamstown, MA, 1970.

___L. G. Miles, THE HESSIANS OF LEWIS MILLER, Precision Printers, Millvale, PA, 1983.

___H. Radloff and A. Coyle, HESSIANS IN THE REVOLUTION, 1776-83, St. Louis Genealogical Society, St. Louis, MO, 1975.

___H. H. Rimpau, THE BRUNSWICK MERCENARIES IN NORTH AMERICA, Archiv fur Sippenforschung, volume 37, 1971, pp. 204-19, 293-308, and volume 38, 1972, pp. 346-55. [About 1700 German soldiers failing to return to Europe]; see also IL State Genealogical Quarterly, volume 6, 1974, pp. 77-81.

___J. G. Rosengarten, THE GERMAN SOLDIER IN THE WARS OF THE US, Lippincott, Philadelphia, PA, 1890.

___C. N. Smith, BRITISH AND GERMAN DESERTERS, DISCHARGES, AND PRISONERS OF WAR WHO MAY HAVE REMAINED IN CANADA AND THE US, 1774-83, Westland Publications, McNeal, AZ, 1991.

___C. N. Smith, BRUNSWICK DESERTER-IMMIGRANTS OF THE AMERICAN REVOLUTION, Heritage House, Thomson, IL, 1973. [About 3000 names.]

___C. N. Smith, DESERTERS AND DISBANDED SOLDIERS FROM BRITISH, GERMAN, AND LOYALIST MILITARY UNITS IN THE SOUTH, 1782, Westland Publications, McNeal, AZ, 1991.

___C. N. Smith, ENCYCLOPEDIA OF GERMAN-AMERICAN GENEALOGICAL RESEARCH, Bowker, New York, NY, 1976, pp. 202-5.

___C. N. Smith, MERCENARIES FROM ANSBACH AND BEYREUTH WHO REMAINED IN AMERICA AFTER THE REVOLUTION, Heritage House, Thomson, IL, 1974.

___C. N. Smith, MERCENARIES FROM HESSEN-HANAU WHO REMAINED IN CANADA AND THE US, Westland Publications, McNeal, AZ, 1984.

___C. N. Smith, MUSTER ROLLS AND PRISONER-OF-WAR LISTS IN AMERICAN ARCHIVES PERTAINING TO THE GERMAN MERCENARY TROOPS, Heritage House, Thomson, IL, 1975.

___C. N. Smith, NOTES ON HESSIAN SOLDIERS WHO REMAINED IN CANADA AND THE US AFTER THE AMERICAN REVOLUTION, Westland Publications, McNeal, AZ, 1992.

___E. Stadtler, DIE ANSBACH-BAYREUTHER TRUPPEN IN AMERIKANSICHEN UNABHANGIGKEITSKRIEG, Kommissions-verlag, die Egge, Nurnberg, 1956. [Lists of German mercenaries.]

___M. H. Volm, THE HESSIAN PRISONERS IN THE AMERICAN WAR OF INDEPENDENCE, Charlottesville, VA, 1937.

Chapter 4

STATE PUBLICATIONS

■■■■■■■ Not only are there publications of lists of
1. Introduction Revolutionary War participants on the national level,
quite a large number of published materials providing
■■■■■■■ lists, rosters, service records, pension rolls, and other
records are available for the thirteen original states.
Published bounty land records for GA, MD, MA, NY, NC, PA, SC, and
VA are also available. It is exceptionally important that you examine
these records, because states often have information on veterans for whom
no mention is made in federal records. State records also often provide
further detail on ancestors mentioned in the national records. Therefore,
if you know or suspect the state from which your ancestor served, it will
generally be informative for you to examine the records of that state. In
section 4 of Chapter 2, we recommended that you contact the archives,
state libraries, and historical societies in these states regarding their
holdings. Here in the next four sections (sections 2-5) of this chapter, we
will list for you important published volumes on each original state. These
volumes can often be located in larger genealogical libraries outside the
state areas, and can usually be located in many libraries, both medium and
large, within the state and in its surrounding area.

■■■■■■■ The colony of CT on 13 July 1774 appointed
2. CT, DE, and GA delegates to the First Continental Congress. This
body, composed of 56 delegates from 12
■■■■■■■ colonies, was the predecessor of the Second
Continental Congress which initiated the actions
leading to American independence. Even though no major land battles
occurred in CT, her coastline cities were the object of naval attacks and
many raids. The state contributed almost 32,000 men to the Continental
Army and over 7200 served in her militia. Works dealing with the CT
forces include:

___A. C. Bates, LISTS AND RETURNS OF CT MEN IN THE
REVOLUTION, CT Historical Society, Hartford, CT, 1909.

___A. C. Bates, ROLLS AND LISTS OF CT MEN IN THE REVOLU-
TION, CT Historical Society, Hartford, CT, 1901.

___T. S. Collier, REVOLUTIONARY PRIVATEERS OF CT, Records
and Papers of the New London County Historical Society, volume 1,
part 4, New London, CT, 1892.

___CT DAR, CT REVOLUTIONARY PENSIONERS, Genealogical

Publishing Co., Baltimore, MD, 1919 (1982).

___CT Historical Society, ROLLS AND LISTS OF CT MEN IN THE REVOLUTION, 1775-1783, The Society, Hartford, CT, 1901.

___CT Sons of the American Revolution, REVOLUTIONARY CHARACTERS OF NEW HAVEN, The Sons, New Haven, CT, 1911. [1000 names.]

___Mrs. A. G. Draper, PENSION RECORDS OF REVOLUTIONARY SOLDIERS FROM CT, 21st Annual Report of the DAR, The Society, Washington, DC, 1919. [11,000 names.]

___J. T. Hayes, CT'S REVOLUTIONARY CAVALRY, Pequot, Chester, CT, 1975.

___J. S. Hedden, CT SOLDIERS OF 1776-83 BURIED IN NEW HAVEN, CT Sons of the American Revolution, New Haven, CT, 1931-4.

___H. P. Johnston, RECORD OF SERVICE OF CT MEN IN THE WAR OF THE REVOLUTION, CT Adjutant General's Office, Hartford, CT, 1889. [30,000 names.]

___F. G. Mather, THE REFUGEES OF 1776 FROM LONG ISLAND TO CT, Lyon, Albany, NY, 1913. [About 18,000 names, including over 2300 refugees.]

___L. F. Middlebrook, HISTORY OF MARITIME CT DURING THE AMERICAN REVOLUTION, Essex Institute, Salem, MA, 1925, 2 volumes.

___M. M. Richardson, and J. J. Mize, 1832 CHEROKEE LAND LOTTERY: INDEX TO REVOLUTIONARY SOLDIERS, THEIR WIDOWS AND ORPHANS WHO WERE FORTUNATE DRAWERS. Taken from Cherokee Land Lottery by James F. Smith, 1838, Heritage Papers, Danielsville, CT, 1969.

___D. O. White, CTs BLACK SOLDIERS, 1775-1783, CT Bicentennial Series, No. 4, Pequot Press, Chester, CT, 1973.

Records pertaining to CT Loyalists include:

___J. Tyler, CT LOYALISTS, Polyanthos, New Orleans, LA, 1979.

The colony of DE on 01 August 1774 appointed delegates to the First Continental Congress. It was the first of the colonies to ratify the Constitution. Only one small skirmish-type encounter took place in DE, that being the battle at Cooch's Bridge (03 September 1777). The state sent over 2300 men into the Continental Army and almost 400 served in her militia. Some works which may be consulted are:

___H. H. Bellas, A HISTORY OF THE DE STATE SOCIETY OF THE CINCINNATI, Historical Society of DE, Wilmington, DE, 1895. [Officers names, brief regimental histories.]

___DE Public Archives Commission, DE ARCHIVES: COLONIAL AND
REVOLUTIONARY WAR, AMS Press, New York, NY, 1974,
volumes 1-3. [Index in volume 3, over 5000 men.]
___C. L. Ward, THE DE CONTINENTALS, 1776-83, The Author,
Wilmington, DE, 1941. [Rosters of officers, index of persons.]
___W. G. Whiteley, THE REVOLUTIONARY SOLDIERS OF DE,
Historical Society of DE, Wilmington, DE, 1896.
For DE Loyalists, see:
___H. B. Hancock, THE DE LOYALISTS, Historical Society of DE,
Wilmington, DE, 1940.

The colony of GA, though absent from the First Continental Congress,
sent delegates to the Second. The major city of GA, Savannah, fell to the
British on 29 December 1778 and remained occupied until the end of the
War, giving the English forces virtual control of coastal GA even though
the interior was never under complete subdual. Two actions of some
consequence should be noted, the failure of an American-French force to
take Savannah in an unsuccessful seige running from 03 September
through 26 October 1779, and the Battle of Kettle Creek near
Washington, GA, on 14 February 1779. Almost 2700 men were sent into
the Continental Army by GA. Among the better works relating to GA
servicemen are these:
___R. Blair, REVOLUTIONARY SOLDIERS' RECEIPTS FOR GA
BOUNTY LAND GRANTS, Foote & Davis, Atlanta, GA, 1928.
[About 1000 names.]
___N. Brawner, DAR OF GA MEMBERSHIP ROLL AND REGISTER,
The Author, Atlanta, GA, 1946. [About 2500 ancestors.]
___A. D. Candler, REVOLUTIONARY RECORDS OF GA, AMS Press,
New York, NY, 1908, 3 volumes.
___DAR OF GA, HISTORIES OF REVOLUTIONARY SOLDIERS,
The Society, Atlanta, GA, 2 typescript volumes. [Over 500 names.]
___R. S. Davis, Jr., CITIZENS AND SOLDIERS OF THE AMERICAN
REVOLUTION, Southern Historical Press, Easley, SC, 1979. [Over
4800 listings.]
___A. M. Hitz, AUTHENTIC LIST OF ALL LAND LOTTERY
GRANTS MADE TO VETERANS OF THE WAR BY GA, GA
Secretary of State, Atlanta, GA, 1955.
___M. L. Houston, REPRINT OF OFFICIAL REGISTER OF LAND
LOTTERY OF GA, Genealogical Publishing Co., Baltimore, MD,
1967. [About 1500 names.]
___M. L. Houston, REVOLUTIONARY SOLDIERS AND WIDOWS
LIVING IN GA, 1827-8, Heritage Papers, Danielsville, GA, 1965.

__L. L. Knight, GA'S ROSTER OF THE REVOLUTION, Index Printing Co., Atlanta, GA, 1920. [9000 names.]

__E. T. McCall, ROSTER OF REVOLUTIONARY SOLDIERS IN GA, Genealogical Publishing Co., Baltimore, MD, 1968-9, 3 volumes. [Over 19,000 listings of veterans and descendants; exercise caution when using.]

__ROLL OF OFFICERS AND MEMBERS OF THE GA HUSSARS AND CAVALRY COMPANIES, Morning News, Savannah, GA, 1906.

__J. F. Smith, THE CHEROKEE LAND LOTTERY CONTAINING A NUMERICAL LIST OF FORTUNATE DRAWERS, Genealogical Publishing Co., Baltimore, MD, 1969. [Over 700 soldiers' names.]

Records of Loyalists in GA are as follows:

__A. D. Candler, REVOLUTIONARY RECORDS OF GA, AMS Press, New York, NY, 1908, 3 volumes. Confiscated estates.

__M. J. Clark, LOYALISTS IN THE SOUTHERN CAMPAIGN OF THE REVOLUTIONARY WAR, Genealogical Publishing Co., Baltimore, MD, 1981, volume 1.

__R. S. Davis, Jr., GA CITIZENS AND SOLDIERS OF THE AMERICAN REVOLUTION, Southern Historical Press, Easley, SC, 1979.

__L. F. Hays, GA MILITARY RECORDS, 1779-1842, 9 typescript volumes, GA State Archives, Atlanta, GA.

__AN INDEX TO GA COLONIAL CONVEYANCES AND CONFISCATED LANDS RECORDS, Taylor Foundation, Atlanta, GA, 1981.

__L. Parrish, RECORDS OF SOME SOUTHERN LOYALISTS, microfilm of manuscript, GA State Archives, Atlanta, GA.

3. MD, MA, and NH

The colony of MD chose its delegates to the First Continental Congress on 25 June 1774. No military action of any consequence was seen in MD during the Revolution. However, soldiers from MD fought in practically every major battle. Almost 14,000 men were contributed to the Continental Army and over 3900 militia fought. Most important among the books listing MD veterans are:

__J. M. Brewer and L. Meyer, THE LAWS AND RULES OF THE LAND OFFICES OF MD, The Offices, Baltimore, MD, 1871. [Land given to MD soldiers.]

__G. M. Brumbaugh, MD RECORDS: COLONIAL, REVO-LUTIONARY, COUNTY, AND CHURCH, From Original Sources,

Williams & Wilkins, Baltimore, MD, 1915. Reprint, Genealogical Publishing Co., Baltimore, MD, 1985.

___G. M. Brumbaugh and M. R. Hodges, REVOLUTIONARY RECORDS OF MD, Genealogical Publishing Co., Baltimore, MD, 1924. [About 5000 names.]

___A. W. Burns, MD SOLDIERS OF THE REVOLUTIONARY, 1812, AND INDIAN WARS WHO DREW PENSIONS IN KY, Washington, DC, no date.

___B. S. Carothers, SIGNERS OF OATHS OF FIDELITY TO MD DURING THE REVOLUTION, The Author, Lutherville, MD, 1975-8, 2 volumes.

___MD Hall of Records Commission, CALENDAR OF MD STATE PAPERS, The Commission, Annapolis, MD, 1943/50, numbers 3 and 4.

___MD Hall of Records Commission, CATALOG OF ARCHIVAL MATERIAL, The Commission, Annapolis, MD, 1942.

___MD Historical Society, MUSTER ROLLS AND OTHER RECORDS OF SERVICE OF MD TROOPS IN THE AMERICAN REVOLUTION, Archives of MD, Baltimore, MD, 1900. [Over 20,000 listings.]

___L. K. McGhee, MD PENSION ABSTRACTS: REVOLUTIONARY, 1812, AND INDIAN WARS, Washington, DC, 1966.

___L. K. McGhee, MD REVOLUTIONARY WAR PENSIONERS, WAR OF 1812, AND INDIAN WARS, Washington, DC, 1952.

___L. K. McGhee, PENSION ABSTRACTS OF MD SOLDIERS WHO SETTLED IN KY, The Author, Washington, DC, no date.

___O. E. Monnette and L. L. French, SPIRIT OF PATRIOTISM, CA Sons of the American Revolution, Los Angeles, CA, 1915. [Thousands of MD soldiers.]

___M. Motsinger, DIRECTORY OF MD DAR AND THEIR REVOLUTIONARY ANCESTORS, The DAR, Bel Air, MD, 1966.

___H. W. Newman, MD REVOLUTIONARY RECORDS, Genealogical Publishing Co., Baltimore, MD, 1967. [Over 3800 names.]

___R. Steuart, A HISTORY OF THE MD LINE IN THE REVOLUTIONARY WAR, Society of the Cincinnati of MD, Baltimore, MD, 1969. [Officer lists, biographical sketches.]

Some MD Loyalist records will be found in:

___M. J. Clark, LOYALISTS IN THE SOUTHERN CAMPAIGN OF THE REVOLUTIONARY WAR, Genealogical Publishing Co., Baltimore, MD, 1981, volume 2.

___ORDERLY BOOK OF THE MD LOYALISTS REGIMENT, Historical Printing Club, Brooklyn, NY, 1891.

The colony of MA declared its indeendence of Britain on 10 May 1776 and on 17 June 1774 chose its delegates to the First Continental Congress. It was in this colony that the inaugurating phases of the Revolution took place. MA contributed the largest number to the Continental Army of any of the colonies, namely, almost 68,000 men. In addition, over 15,000 militia were involved. Records of these servicemen are to be found in:

___G. W. Allen, MA PRIVATEERS OF THE REVOLUTION, MA Historical Society, Boston, MA, 1927. [Vessels, commanders, owners.]

___F. W. Coburn, THE BATTLE OF APRIL 19, 1775 IN LEXINGTON, The Author, Lexington, MA, 1912. [3600 names.]

___B. M. Draper, HONOR ROLL OF MA PATRIOTS WHO LOANED MONEY TO THE FEDERAL GOVERNMENT, Boston, MA, no Publisher or date available.

___C. A. Flagg, AN ALPHABETICAL LIST OF REVOLUTIONARY PENSIONERS LIVING IN ME, Genealogical Publishing Co., Baltimore, MD, 1920. [Many MA soldiers included.]

___C. E. Hambrick-Stowe and D. Smerlas, MA MILITIA COMPANIES AND OFFICERS OF THE LEXINGTON ALARM, New England Historic Genealogical Society, Boston, MA, 1976.

___Mrs. L. Irwin, DIRECTORY OF MEMBERS AND ANCESTORS, DAR OF MA, Newton, MA, 1974. [About 2800 ancestors.]

___MA Secretary of the Commonwealth, MA SOLDIERS AND SAILORS OF THE REVOLUTIONARY WAR, Wright and Potter, Boston, MA, 1896-1908, 17 volumes. [About 170,000 entries, many duplicates, incomplete.]

___MA Society of the Cincinnati, MEMORIALS OF THE MA SOCIETY OF THE CINCINNATI, The Society, Boston, MA, 1873/1890/1931/1964.

___L. K. McGhee, MA PENSION ABSTRACTS OF THE REVOLUTIONARY, 1812, AND INDIAN WARS, The Author, Washington, DC, 1966.

___C. C. Tucker, A LIST OF PENSIONERS IN THE STATE OF MA, Polkinhorn, Washington, DC, 1854. [3800 names.]

There are also several volumes listing Loyalists in the state:

___J. T. Hassam, THE CONFISCATED ESTATES OF BOSTON LOYALISTS, Wilson and Sons, Cambridge, MA, 1895.

___E. A. Jones, THE LOYALISTS OF MA, Genealogical Publishing Co., Baltimore, MD, 1969. [Over 600 biographies.]

___D. E. Maas, DIVIDED HEARTS: MA LOYALISTS, 1765-90, New England Historic Genealogical Society, Boston, MA, 1980.

___J. H. Stark, THE LOYALISTS OF MA, Kelley, Clifton, NJ, 1910. [Over 2000 names.]

The colony of NH selected its First Continental Congressional delegation on 21 June 1774. Although no military action of any moment took place in NH, the state supplied about 12,500 men for service in the Continental Army, and about 3700 militia were involved at one time or another. Recommended works for your perusal if your ancestor was from NH are:

___A. S. Batchellor, MISCELLANEOUS REVOLUTIONARY DOCUMENTS OF NH, PROVINCIAL AND STATE PAPERS OF NH, State of NH, Manchester, NH, 1910, volume 30.

___DAR OF NH, DIRECTORY OF MEMBERS AND ANCESTORS, The Society, Littleton, NH, 1964.

___Mrs. A. G. Draper and Mrs. M. L. Driscoll, NH REVOLUTIONARY PENSIONERS, National Genealogical Society Quarterly, 1922-40, volumes 11-29.

___G. C. Gilmore, NH MEN AT BUNKER HILL, Secretary of State of NH, MANUAL FOR THE GENERAL COURT, No. 6, 1899, pp. 29-86. [About 1700 names.]

___G. C. Gilmore, ROLL OF NH SOLDIERS AT THE BATTLE OF BENNINGTON, State of NH, Manchester, 1891. [About 1500 names.]

___I. W. Hammond, ROLLS OF THE SOLDIERS IN THE REVOLUTIONARY WAR, PROVINCIAL AND STATE PAPERS OF NH, AMS Press, New York, NY, 1973, volumes 14-17, 30.

___NH PENSION NAME INDEX, NH Historical Society, Concord, NH, 71 volumes.

___C. E. Potter, MILITARY HISTORY OF THE STATE OF NH, 1623-1861, Genealogical Publishing Co., Baltimore, MD, 1972.

Some useful materials treating Loyalists are:

___O. G. Hammond, TORIES OF NH IN THE WAR OF THE REVOLUTION, Gregg Press, Boston, MA, 1972.

___NH LOYALISTS, Public Record Office, London, no date, 5 volumes; copy in NH State Library, Concord, NH.

4. NJ, NY, and NC

The colony of NJ acted to constitute its delegation to the First Continental Congress on 23 July 1774. The state has often been referred to as the cockpit of the Revolution because its position between New York and Philadelphia saw troops of both sides moving back and forth across it and engaging in over three critical battles. NJ gave almost 12,000 soldiers to the Continental Army and fielded over 4400 militiamen. Books which will be important for the tracing of a NJ Revolutionary War ancestor include:

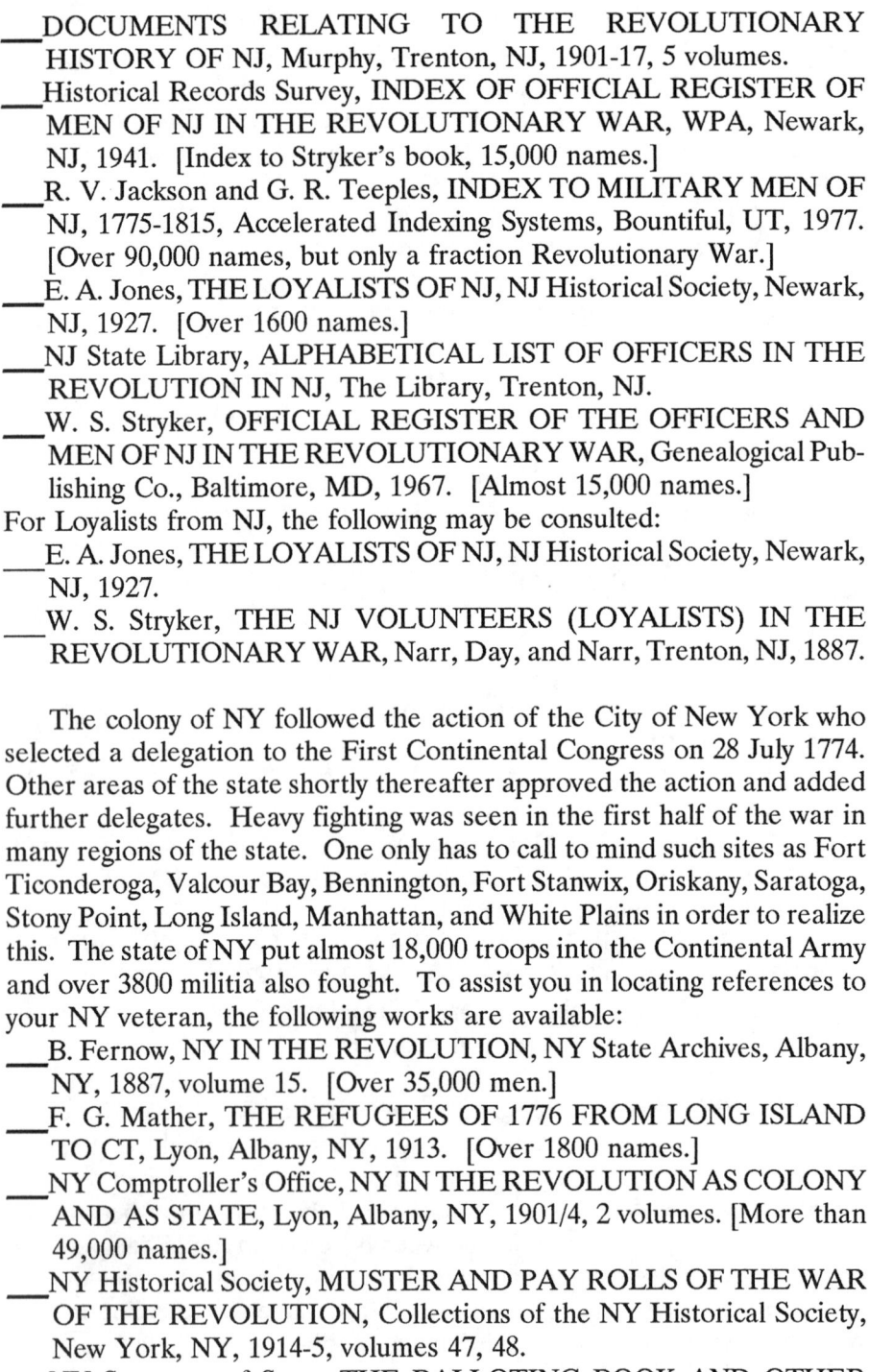

___DOCUMENTS RELATING TO THE REVOLUTIONARY HISTORY OF NJ, Murphy, Trenton, NJ, 1901-17, 5 volumes.

___Historical Records Survey, INDEX OF OFFICIAL REGISTER OF MEN OF NJ IN THE REVOLUTIONARY WAR, WPA, Newark, NJ, 1941. [Index to Stryker's book, 15,000 names.]

___R. V. Jackson and G. R. Teeples, INDEX TO MILITARY MEN OF NJ, 1775-1815, Accelerated Indexing Systems, Bountiful, UT, 1977. [Over 90,000 names, but only a fraction Revolutionary War.]

___E. A. Jones, THE LOYALISTS OF NJ, NJ Historical Society, Newark, NJ, 1927. [Over 1600 names.]

___NJ State Library, ALPHABETICAL LIST OF OFFICERS IN THE REVOLUTION IN NJ, The Library, Trenton, NJ.

___W. S. Stryker, OFFICIAL REGISTER OF THE OFFICERS AND MEN OF NJ IN THE REVOLUTIONARY WAR, Genealogical Publishing Co., Baltimore, MD, 1967. [Almost 15,000 names.]

For Loyalists from NJ, the following may be consulted:

___E. A. Jones, THE LOYALISTS OF NJ, NJ Historical Society, Newark, NJ, 1927.

___W. S. Stryker, THE NJ VOLUNTEERS (LOYALISTS) IN THE REVOLUTIONARY WAR, Narr, Day, and Narr, Trenton, NJ, 1887.

The colony of NY followed the action of the City of New York who selected a delegation to the First Continental Congress on 28 July 1774. Other areas of the state shortly thereafter approved the action and added further delegates. Heavy fighting was seen in the first half of the war in many regions of the state. One only has to call to mind such sites as Fort Ticonderoga, Valcour Bay, Bennington, Fort Stanwix, Oriskany, Saratoga, Stony Point, Long Island, Manhattan, and White Plains in order to realize this. The state of NY put almost 18,000 troops into the Continental Army and over 3800 militia also fought. To assist you in locating references to your NY veteran, the following works are available:

___B. Fernow, NY IN THE REVOLUTION, NY State Archives, Albany, NY, 1887, volume 15. [Over 35,000 men.]

___F. G. Mather, THE REFUGEES OF 1776 FROM LONG ISLAND TO CT, Lyon, Albany, NY, 1913. [Over 1800 names.]

___NY Comptroller's Office, NY IN THE REVOLUTION AS COLONY AND AS STATE, Lyon, Albany, NY, 1901/4, 2 volumes. [More than 49,000 names.]

___NY Historical Society, MUSTER AND PAY ROLLS OF THE WAR OF THE REVOLUTION, Collections of the NY Historical Society, New York, NY, 1914-5, volumes 47, 48.

___NY Secretary of State, THE BALLOTING BOOK AND OTHER

DOCUMENTS RELATING TO MILITARY BOUNTY LANDS IN NY, The Secretary, Albany, NY, 1825.

___NY Secretary of State, CALENDAR OF HISTORICAL MANU-SCRIPTS RELATING TO THE WAR OF THE REVOLUTION IN THE OFFICE OF THE SECRETARY OF STATE, The Secretary, Albany, NY, 1968, 2 volumes.

___NY State Committee of Historical Research and Preservations, GRAVE RECORDS OF REVOLUTIONARY SOLDIERS BURIED IN NY, The Committee, New York, NY, 1938, 11 volumes.

Books dealing with Loyalists in the state of NY are:

___A. C. Flick, LOYALISM IN NY DURING THE AMERICAN REVOLUTION, AMS Press, New York, NY, 1970.

___W. Kelby, LOYALISTS: ORDERLY BOOK OF THE THREE BAT-TALIONS OF DELANCEY AND A LIST OF NY CITY LOYALISTS, Genealogical Publishing Co., Baltimore, MD, 1972. [Over 1500 New York City Loyalists.]

___NY CITY DURING THE AMERICAN REVOLUTION, NY Mercantile Library Association, New York, NY, 1861.

___NY Historical Society, MINUTES OF THE COMMITTEE AND OF THE FIRST COMMISSION FOR DETECTING AND DEFEATING CONSPIRACIES IN NY, Collections of the NY Historical Society, New York, NY, 1924-5, 2 volumes.

___K. Scott, RIVINGTONS NY NEWSPAPER: EXCERPTS FROM A LOYALIST PRESS, 1773-83, NY Historical Society, New York, NY, 1973.

___H. B. Yoshpe, THE DISPOSITION OF LOYALIST ESTATES IN THE SOUTHERN DISTRICT OF NY, Columbia Univ. Press, New York, NY, 1939.

The colony of NC chose their delegation to the First Continental Congress on 25 August 1774. Early in the War there was considerable internal strife, but British forces did not do battle in NC until the latter half of the war, chiefly when Cornwallis came up through the state from SC. NC soldiers in the Continental Army numbered a little over 7000 and almost 4000 militia fought on the home front. Among important documents for searching out your NC Revolutionary ancestor are:

___G. M. Battey, THE TN BEE-HIVE: EARLY NC GRANTS IN THE VOLUNTEER STATE, 1778-91, Library of Congress, Washington, DC, 1849.

___A. Blair, A LIST OF REVOLUTIONARY SOLDIERS BURIED IN NC, Historical Collections of GA Chapters, DAR, volume 1, 1926, pp. 352-64.

___A. W. Burns, ABSTRACTS OF PENSIONS OF NC SOLDIERS IN THE REVOLUTIONARY, 1812, AND INDIAN WARS, The Author, Washington, DC, 1960-4.

___G. F. Burgner, compiler, NC LAND GRANTS IN TN, 1778-91, Southern Historical Press, Easley, SC, 1981. [Almost 6000 names.]

___B. J. Camin, NC REVOLUTIONARY WAR PENSION APPLICATIONS, 3 vols., Southern Historical Press, Raleigh, NC, 1981.

___W. Clark, ROSTER OF CONTINENTAL LINE FROM NC, State Records of NC, volume 16, pp. 1002-1197. [Over 4700 names.]

___DAR of NC, MEMBERS AND ANCESTORS, Dunn, New Bern, NC, 1948. [Over 2400 ancestors.]

___DAR of NC, ROSTER OF SOLDIERS FROM NC IN THE AMERICAN REVOLUTION, The Society, Durham, NC, 1932. [About 36,000 names, including many thousand soldiers.]

___DAR of TN, ROSTER OF TN SOLDIERS IN THE REVOLUTION LIVING IN THE COUNTIES OF WASHINGTON AND SULLIVAN, The Society, Bristol, TN, 1935. [1500 names, these counties were in NC then.]

___C. L. Davis, A BRIEF HISTORY OF THE NC TROOPS ON THE CONTINENTAL ESTABLISHMENT, Philadelphia, PA, 1896. [About 500 officers.]

___W. P. Haun, NC REVOLUTIONARY ARMY ACCOUNTS: SECRETARY OF STATE, TRASURER S AND COMPTROLLER S PAPERS, 5 vols, 2nd ed., The Author, Durham, NC, 1988-90.

___J. T. Maddox and M. Carter, NC REVOLUTIONARY SOLDIERS, SAILORS, AND PATRIOTS, GA Pioneers, Albany, GA, 1979, 2 volumes. [Over 5500 names.]

___NC'S REVOLUTIONARY WAR PAY RECORDS, NC Division of Archives Information Circular No. 1, Raleigh, NC, 1973.

___THE STATE RECORDS OF NC, Nash, Goldsboro, NC, 1886-1907, 30 volumes. [See volume 16 and indexes in volumes 4, 27-30 for rosters.]

___G. Stevenson, NC REVOLUTIONARY WAR RECORDS OF PRIMARY INTEREST TO GENEALOGISTS, NC Division of Archives Information Circular No. 13, Raleigh, NC, 1974.

Materials dealing with the British and Loyalists are also available:

___M. J. Clark, LOYALISTS IN THE SOUTHERN CAMPAIGN OF THE REVOLUTIONARY WAR, Genealogical Publishing Co., Baltimore, MD, 1981, volume 1.

___R. O. Demond, LOYALISTS IN NC DURING THE REVOLUTION, Genealogical Publishing Co., Baltimore, MD, 1979. [Lists of Loyalists.]

___A. B. Pruitt, ABSTRACTS OF SALES OF CONFISCATED
LOYALIST LAND AND PROPERTY IN NC, The Author, Raleigh,
NC, 1989.

___D. Schenk, NC, 1780-1, A HISTORY OF THE INVASION OF THE
CAROLINAS BY THE BRITISH ARMY, Edwards and Broughton,
Raleigh, NC, 1889. [About 1000 officers.]

5. PA, RI, SC, and VA

The colony of PA elected its delegates to the First Continental Congress on 22 July 1774. This state was the scene of the first two Continental Congresses, and in 1777 battles were fought at Brandywine, Paoli, Fort Mifflin, and Germantown. During the enemy occupation of Philadelphia, two other PA cities served as sites of the Continental Congress: Lancaster and York. Almost 26,000 PA soldiers served in the Continental Army and over 7300 fought in the militia. The most useful works for seeking records of a PA veteran are:

___W. H. Egle, PA IN THE WAR OF THE REVOLUTION,
ASSOCIATED BATTALIONS AND MILITIA, Meyers, Harrisburg,
PA, 1887-8, 2 volumes.

___F. G. Hoenstine, 1955 YEARBOOK OF THE SONS OF THE
AMERICAN REVOLUTION, The Sons, Pittsburgh, PA, 1956. [7000
names.]

___J. B. Linn and W. Egle, PA IN THE WAR OF THE REVOLUTION:
BATTALIONS AND LINE, 1775-83, Hart, Harrisburg, PA, 1880.

___L. K. McGhee, PA PENSION ABSTRACTS OF SOLDIERS IN THE
REVOLUTIONARY, 1812, AND INDIAN WARS, The Author,
Washington, DC, no date.

___PA ARCHIVES, 2nd Series (volumes 1, 3, 8-11, 13-15), 3rd Series
(volumes 3, 5-7, 23), 5th Series (volumes 1-8), 6th Series (volumes 1,
2, 15, and index to 6th Series), PA Historical and Museum
Commission, Harrisburg, PA, 1949; to be used with H. H. Eddy and
M. Simonetti, GUIDE TO THE PUBLISHED ARCHIVES OF PA,
PA Historical and Museum Commission, Harrisburg, PA, 1976.

___H. M. M. Richards, PA-GERMANS IN THE REVOLUTIONARY
WAR, Genealogical Publishing Co., Baltimore, MD, 1978. [About
1500 surnames.]

___T. Westcott, NAMES OF PERSONS WHO TOOK THE OATH OF
ALLEGIANCE TO PA, 1777-89, Campbell, Philadelphia, PA, 1865.

Among the better works for PA Loyalist listings are:

___M. J. Clark, LOYALISTS IN THE SOUTHERN CAMPAIGN OF
THE REVOLUTIONARY WAR, Genealogical Publishing Co.,

Baltimore, MD, 1981, volume 2.
___T. L. Montgomery, FORFEITED ESTATES INVENTORIES AND SALES, Harrisburg Publ. Co., Harrisburg, PA, 1907.

The colony of RI selected its delegates for the First Continental Congress on 15 June 1774. This little colony had long resisted the British taxation regulations. Almost 6000 of her men belonged to the Continental Army and more than 4200 militiamen were active. With the exception of the Battle of RI at Newport on 29 August 1778, no engagements of any great import were carried out on the state's soil. The books of greatest utility to you in looking for records of your ancestor's RI service are:
___B. Cowell, SPIRIT OF 76 IN RI, Genealogical Publishing Co., Baltimore, MD, 1973. [Many officers and men.]
___National Society of the DAR, MINORITY MILITARY SERVICE, RI, 1775-1783, DAR, Washington, DC, 1988. Participation of African-Americans in the American Revolution, includes name, year, and source.
___T. H. Murray, IRISH RHODE ISLANDERS IN THE AMERICAN REVOLUTION, American-Irish Historical Society, Providence, RI, 1903.
___RI Adjutant Generals Office, NAMES OF OFFICERS, SOLDIERS AND SEAMEN IN RI REGIMENTS, OR BELONGING TO THE STATE OF RI, AND SERVICE IN THE REGIMENTS OF OTHER STATES AND IN THE REGULAR ARMY AND NAVY OF THE US, WHO LOST THEIR LIVES IN THE DEFENCE OF THEIR COUNTRY IN THE SUPPRESSION OF THE LATE REBELLION, Providence Press, Providence, RI, 1869.
___J. J. Smith, CIVIL AND MILITARY LISTS OF RI, 1647-1850, Preston and Rounds, Providence, RI, 1900-7, 3 volumes.
___A. Walker, SO FEW THE BRAVE: RI CONTINENTALS,1775-1783, Seafield Press, East Greenwich, RI, RI Society, Sons of the American Revolution, 1981.

The colony of SC on 02 August 1774 selected its delegates to be sent to the First Continental Congress. SC saw 188 battles fought within its borders. The state was a constant hot-bed of military activity throughout the War, much of the conflict taking the proportions of a civil war with patriots and loyalists continually at each other. More than 6000 soldiers were put into the Continental Army by SC, and many militia took the field. Recommended volumes for your information quest on a SC Revolutionary War ancestor are:
___J. D. Bailey, SOME HEROES OF THE AMERICAN

REVOLUTION, Southern Historical Press, Easley, SC, 1924.

___W. W. Boddie, MARION'S MEN, A LIST OF 2500, The Author, Charleston, SC, 1938. [Over 2500 listings.]

___A. W. Burns, SC PENSION ABSTRACTS OF THE REVOLUTIONARY, 1812, AND INDIAN WARS, The Author, Washington, DC, no date.

___Commission of the Navy Board, JOURNAL OF THE COMMISSIONERS OF THE NAVY OF SC: 1776-80, Historical Commission of SC, Columbia, SC, 1912-13.

___W. G. De Saussure, THE NAMES OF THE OFFICERS WHO SERVED IN THE SC REGIMENTS ON THE CONTINENTAL ESTABLISHMENT AND IN THE MILITIA, Yearbook 1893, Charleston, SC, pp. 205-37.

___S. S. Ervin, SOUTH CAROLINIANS IN THE REVOLUTION, Genealogical Publishing Co., Baltimore, MD, 1971. [About 2500 names.]

___Mrs. G. D. Foxworth, ROSTER AND ANCESTRAL ROLL, DAR of SC, Columbia, SC, 1954. [Over 2000 ancestors.]

___Mrs. F. C. Hensley, RECORDS OF REVOLUTIONARY WAR SOL-DIERS BURIED IN SC, DAR of SC, and Library, University of SC, Columbia, SC, 1967-70.

___J. T. Maddox and M. Carter, SC REVOLUTIONARY SOLDIERS, SAILORS, PATRIOTS, AND DESCENDANTS, GA Pioneers Publi-cations, Albany, GA, 1975. [Almost 1000 veterans.]

___O. E. Monnette and L. L. French, SPIRIT OF PATRIOTISM AS EVIDENCED BY THE REVOLUTIONARY AND ANCESTRAL RECORDS OF THE SOCIETY, CA Sons of the American Revolution, Los Angeles, CA, 1915. [Thousands of names.]

___B. G. Moss, ROSTER OF SC PATRIOTS IN THE AMERICAN REVOLUTION, Genealogical Publishing Co., Baltimore, MD, 1982. [Over 20,000 soldiers.]

___J. C. G. Pruitt, REVOLUTIONARY WAR PENSION APPLICANTS WHO SERVED FROM SC, Charlton Hall, Fairfax, VA, 1946.

___J. Revill, REVOLUTIONARY CLAIMS FILED IN SC, 1783-6, Genealogical Publishing Co., Baltimore, MD, 1939. [About 4000 names.]

___A. S. Salley, Jr., DOCUMENTS RELATING TO THE HISTORY OF SC DURING THE REVOLUTIONARY WAR, Historical Commission of SC, Columbia, SC, 1908.

___A. S. Salley, Jr. SC PROVINCIAL TROOPS, Genealogical Publishing Co., Baltimore, MD, 1977. [Several thousand men.]

___A. S. Salley, Jr., RECORDS OF THE REGIMENTS OF THE SC

LINE IN THE REVOLUTIONARY WAR, Genealogical Publishing Co., Baltimore, MD, 1977.

___A. S. Salley, Jr. and W. A. Wates, STUB ENTRIES OF INDENTS ISSUED IN PAYMENT OF CLAIMS AGAINST SC GROWING OUT OF THE REVOLUTION, SC Department of Archives and History, Columbia, SC, 1810-57, 12 volumes. [Over 15000 entries.]

___SC Department of Archives and History, ACCOUNTS AUDITED OF CLAIMS GROWING OUT OF THE REVOLUTION IN SC, The Department, Columbia, SC, Microcopy No. 8, 170 rolls. [About 9000 files.]

For SC Loyalists, you may consult:

___M. J. Clark, LOYALISTS IN THE SOUTHERN CAMPAIGN OF THE REVOLUTIONARY WAR, Genealogical Publishing Co., Baltimore, MD, 1981, volume 1.

The colony of VA on 01 August 1774 chose its delegation for the First Continental Congress. Warfare was pronounced in VA early in the War (patriot and loyalist clashes over Norfolk) and late in the war (particularly the events leading up to the surrender). Just a few less than 27,000 Virginians were members of the Continental Army and over 4000 did militia service. The following books are among the better for you if you know or suspect you had a VA Revolutionary patriot:

___G. M. Brumbaugh, REVOLUTIONARY WAR RECORDS: VA ARMY AND NAVY FORCES WITH BOUNTY LAND WARRANTS, Genealogical Publishing Co., Baltimore, MD, 1967. [About 7000 names.]

___L. A. Burgess, VA SOLDIERS OF 1776, Richmond Press, Richmond, VA, 1927-9, 3 volumes. [Over 10,000 men.]

___W. A. Crozier, VA COLONIAL MILITIA, 1651-1776, Southern Book Co., Baltimore, MD, 1954.

___DAR of VA, ROSTER, 1890-1958, The Society, Pulaski, VA, 1958, also SUPPLEMENT, 1962. [Over 5200 ancestors.]

___J. F. Dorman, VA'S REVOLUTIONARY PENSION APPLICATIONS, ABSTRACTED, The Author, Washington, DC, 1958-, volumes 1-. [Thosands of names in numerous volumes.]

___H. J. Eckenrode, LIST OF REVOLUTIONARY SOLDIERS OF VA, VA State Library, Bottom, Richmond, VA, 1911, with Supplement and 1911 and 1912 Special Reports. [About 43,000 names.]

___M. and L. Gardner, VA REVOLUTIONARY WAR STATE PENSIONS, VA Genealogical Society, Richmond, VA, 1980. [Over 5000 names from over 500 applications.]

___J. H. Gwathmey, HISTORICAL REGISTER OF VIRGINIANS IN

THE REVOLUTION, Dietz, Richmond, VA, 1938. [Over 64,000 names.]

___W. L. Hopkins, VA REVOLUTIONARY WAR LAND GRANT CLAIMS (REJECTED), 1783-1850 (rejected), The Author, abstracted from records at the Virginia State Library, Richmond, VA, 1988.

___W. R. Jillson, THE KY LAND GRANTS; A SYSTEMATIC INDEX TO ALL OF THE LAND GRANTS RECORDED IN THE STATE LAND OFFICE AT FRANKFORT, KY, 1782-1924, Filson Club Publications, No. 33, Louisville, KY, 1925.

___A. Latham and B. G. Leonard, A ROLL OF THE OFFICERS IN THE VA LINE OF THE REVOLUTIONARY ARMY WHO RECEIVED LAND BOUNTY IN OH AND KY, The Authors, Chillicothe, OH, 1822.

___LIST OF OFFICERS, SAILORS, AND MARINES OF THE NAVY OF VA IN THE AMERICAN REVOLUTION, VA Magazine of History and Biography, volume 1, 1894, pp. 64-75. [About 600 names.]

___J. T. McAllister, VA MILITIA IN THE REVOLUTIONARY WAR, McAllister Publishing Co., Hot Springs, VA, 1913.

___L. K. McGhee, VA PENSION ABSTRACTS OF THE REVOLUTIONARY, 1812, AND INDIAN WARS, The Author, Washington, DC, 1953-66.

___W. P. Palmer, CALENDAR OF VA STATE PAPERS AND OTHER MANUSCRIPTS, Richmond, VA, no publisher available, several dates.

___W. T. R. Saffell, RECORDS OF THE REVOLUTIONARY WAR, C. C. Saffell, Baltimore, MD, 1894, to be used with the partial index J. T. McAllister, INDEX TO SAFFELL'S LIST OF VA SOLDIERS IN THE REVOLUTION, McAllister, Hot Springs, VA, 1913.

___R. A. Stewart, THE HISTORY OF VA'S NAVY OF THE REVOLUTION, Mitchell and Hotchkiss, Richmond, VA, 1934. [About 2000 names.]

___L. P. Summers, ANNALS OF SOUTHWEST VA, The Author, Abingdon, VA, 1928. [Almost 2000 names.]

___US General Land Office, REPORT FROM THE SECRETARY OF THE TREASURY SHOWING THE AMOUNT OF LAND SCRIPT ISSUED TO OFFICERS AND MEN OF VA, 23rd Congress, Second Session, 1834, Senate Document 4. [About 900 names.]

___Veteran's Administration, VA HALF PAY AND OTHER RELATED REVOLUTIONARY WAR PENSION APPLICATION FILES, National Archives, Microfilm Publication M910, 18 rolls.

___VA Genealogical Society, VA REVOLUTIONARY WAR STATE

PENSIONS, The Society, Richmond, VA, 1980.

___VA General Assembly, A LIST OF NON-COMMISSIONED OFFICERS AND SOLDIERS, SEAMEN, AND MARINES WHO HAVE NOT RECEIVED BOUNTY LAND, Ye Olde Genealogie Shoppe, Indianapolis, IN, 1975.

___VA MILITARY RECORDS, FROM VIRGINIA MAGAZINE OF HISTORY AND BIOGRAPHY, also the William and Mary College Quarterly, and Tylers Quarterly, Genealogical Publishing Co., Baltimore, MD, 1983. [Includes data from muster rolls, pension records, and other documents.]

___VA State Library, 8TH AND 9TH ANNUAL REPORTS, The Library, Richmond, VA, 1910/1, 1911/2. [Lists of VA Continental soldiers.]

___P. G. Wardell, compiler, VA/WV GENEALOGICAL DATA FROM REVOLUTIONARY WAR PENSION AND BOUNTY LAND WARRANT RECORDS, Heritage Books, Bowie, MD, 1988.

___S. M. Wilson, CATALOGUE OF REVOLUTIONARY SOLDIERS AND SAILORS OF VA TO WHOM LAND BOUNTY WARRANTS WERE GRANTED, Genealogical Publishing Co., Baltimore, MD, 1967. [About 3500 names.]

___S. M. Wilson, VA REVOLUTIONARY LAND BOUNTY WARRANTS, Genealogical Publishing Co., Baltimore, MD, 1953.

Some Loyalist lists from VA will be found in:

___M. J. Clark, LOYALISTS IN THE SOUTHERN CAMPAIGN OF THE REVOLUTIONARY WAR, Genealogical Publishing Co., Baltimore, MD, 1981, volume 2.

6. The later states

Following the Revolutionary War, many veterans joined the general westward movement. Quite a sizable number of these were War participants who had received bounty land as compensation or reward for their services. Therefore, the areas into which they moved often have bounty land records in addition to the bounty land records in the original states. Further, many of the later states have compiled lists of Revolutionary War participants living and/or buried within their borders.

There is another source of Revolutionary War ancestor information which is available from DAR chapters in various later states. The state branches of the DAR have in many cases published lists of their members accompanied by the names of veterans which permitted each member to qualify for her membership. These veterans will, of course, be widely spread over the US, and thus not limited to the state from which the DAR report comes.

Many publications containing these bounty land lists, burial lists, DAR ancestor lists, and a few other lists will be indicated in the remainder of this chapter. It will be useful for you to take a look at those volumes relating to states to which your ancestor moved. Many of these books will usually be found in larger genealogical libraries, but as you get nearer the state involved, your chances of finding them grow better.

▬▬▬▬▬▬▬▬▬ Useful volumes for Revolutionary ancestor
7. AL through IN   searches in <u>AL</u> include:
▬▬▬▬▬▬▬▬▬ ___AL Department of Archives and History, REVOLUTIONARY SOLDIERS IN AL: BEING A LIST OF NAMES, COMPILED FROM AUTHENTIC SOURCES, OF SOLDIERS OF THE AMERICAN REVO-LUTION, WHO RESIDED IN THE STATE OF AL, Brown Printing Co., Montgomery, AL, 1967. [Approximately 500 veterans.]
___AL GENEALOGICAL REGISTER, Tuscaloosa, AL, 1959-68, volumes 1-10. [Many Revolutionary War records.]
___P. J. Gandrud, AL REVOLUTIONARY, 1812, AND INDIAN WAR SOLDIERS SURNAMES, McLane, Hot Springs, AR, 1974-, volume 1-.
___L. M. Julich, ROSTER OF REVOLUTIONARY SOLDIERS AND PATRIOTS IN AL, DAR of AL, Parchment, Montgomery, AL, 1979. [Over 900 soldiers.]
___M. B. Owen, REVOLUTIONARY SOLDIERS IN AL, AL State Archives Bulletin 5, Brown, Montgomery, AL, 1911. [About 500 names.]
___A. R. W. Mell, REVOLUTIONARY SOLDIERS BURIED IN AL, AL Historical Society, Reprint 26, Montgomery, AL, 1904. [30 names.]
___E. W. Thomas, REVOLUTIONARY SOLDIERS IN AL, Willo, Tuscaloosa, AL, 1961. [Over 700 names.]

A work which should not be overlooked if you know or suspect descendants of your veteran moved to <u>AR</u> is:
___R. W. Dhonau, A ROSTER OF THE AR SOCIETY, SONS OF THE AMERICAN REVOLUTION, 1890-1985, AND REGISTER OF ANCESTORS, The Author, Little Rock, AR, 1985.
___D. E. Payne, AR PENSIONERS, 1818-1900: RECORDS OF SOME AR RESIDENTS WHO APPLIED TO THE FEDERAL

GOVERNMENT FOR BENEFITS ARISING FROM SERVICE IN FEDERAL MILITARY ORGANIZATIONS (REVOLUTIONARY WAR, WAR OF 1812, INDIAN AND MEXICAN WARS), Southern Historical Press, Easley, SC, 1985. [Lists nearly 1000 individuals.]

___E. S. Rogers, A ROSTER OF THE AR DAR SOCIETY, 1893-1968, DAR of AR, Rogers, AR, 1968, SUPPLEMENT TO THE ROSTER, DAR of AR, Rogers, AR, 1978. [Long list of ancestors.]

For Revolutionary participants and patriots buried in DC, you should try:

___S. M. Ely, THE DC IN THE AMERICAN REVOLUTION AND PATRIOTS INTERRED IN THE DC OR ARLINGTON, Records of the Columbia Historical Society, volume 21, 1918, pp. 129-54. [About 240 entries.]

If your ancestor moved into FL or you suspect that he did, use:

___J. R. Fritot, PENSION RECORDS OF SOLDIERS OF THE REVOLUTION WHO REMOVED TO FL, DAR of Jacksonville, Jacksonville, FL, 1946. [Over 350 listings.]

___W. H. Siebert, LOYALISTS OF EAST FL, 1775-85, FL State Historical Society, DeLand, FL, 1929, 2 volumes.

Or, for Loyalists of FL, consult:

___M. J. Clark, LOYALISTS IN THE SOUTHERN CAMPAIGN OF THE REVOLUTIONARY WAR, Genealogical Publishing Co., Baltimore, MD, 1981, volume 1.

___W. H. Siebert, LOYALISTS IN EAST FL, 1774-85, FL State Historical Society, DeLand, FL, 1929, 2 volumes.

The two volumes by Wood relating to ID DAR members and their Revolutionary War forebears could be pertinent to your quest:

___C. L. Wood, HISTORY AND REGISTER, DAR of ID, Caldwell, ID, 1936, 1963, 2 volumes.

For IL, several books are of value to you regarding your Revolutionary War participant or his descendants who moved there:

___G. C. Clift, LIST OF OFFICERS OF THE IL REGIMENT AND OF CROCKETT'S REGIMENT WHO HAVE RECEIVED LAND FOR THEIR SERVICES, Sons of the American Revolution, Frankfort, IL, 1962.

___DAR of IL, IL STATE DIRECTORY OF MEMBERS AND ANCESTORS, The Society, Galesburg, IL, 1957 and thereafter intermittently.

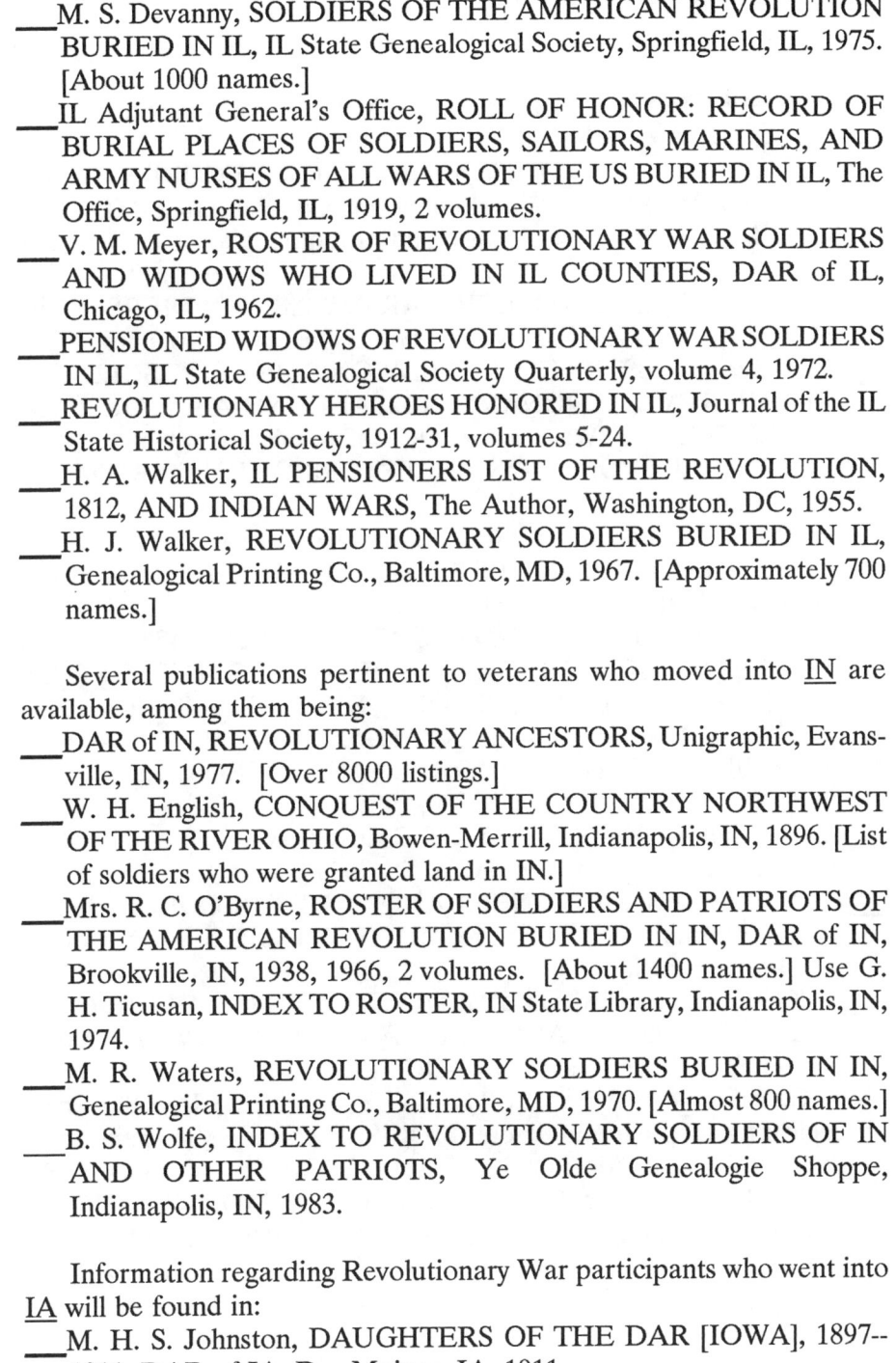

___M. S. Devanny, SOLDIERS OF THE AMERICAN REVOLUTION BURIED IN IL, IL State Genealogical Society, Springfield, IL, 1975. [About 1000 names.]

___IL Adjutant General's Office, ROLL OF HONOR: RECORD OF BURIAL PLACES OF SOLDIERS, SAILORS, MARINES, AND ARMY NURSES OF ALL WARS OF THE US BURIED IN IL, The Office, Springfield, IL, 1919, 2 volumes.

___V. M. Meyer, ROSTER OF REVOLUTIONARY WAR SOLDIERS AND WIDOWS WHO LIVED IN IL COUNTIES, DAR of IL, Chicago, IL, 1962.

___PENSIONED WIDOWS OF REVOLUTIONARY WAR SOLDIERS IN IL, IL State Genealogical Society Quarterly, volume 4, 1972.

___REVOLUTIONARY HEROES HONORED IN IL, Journal of the IL State Historical Society, 1912-31, volumes 5-24.

___H. A. Walker, IL PENSIONERS LIST OF THE REVOLUTION, 1812, AND INDIAN WARS, The Author, Washington, DC, 1955.

___H. J. Walker, REVOLUTIONARY SOLDIERS BURIED IN IL, Genealogical Printing Co., Baltimore, MD, 1967. [Approximately 700 names.]

Several publications pertinent to veterans who moved into IN are available, among them being:

___DAR of IN, REVOLUTIONARY ANCESTORS, Unigraphic, Evansville, IN, 1977. [Over 8000 listings.]

___W. H. English, CONQUEST OF THE COUNTRY NORTHWEST OF THE RIVER OHIO, Bowen-Merrill, Indianapolis, IN, 1896. [List of soldiers who were granted land in IN.]

___Mrs. R. C. O'Byrne, ROSTER OF SOLDIERS AND PATRIOTS OF THE AMERICAN REVOLUTION BURIED IN IN, DAR of IN, Brookville, IN, 1938, 1966, 2 volumes. [About 1400 names.] Use G. H. Ticusan, INDEX TO ROSTER, IN State Library, Indianapolis, IN, 1974.

___M. R. Waters, REVOLUTIONARY SOLDIERS BURIED IN IN, Genealogical Printing Co., Baltimore, MD, 1970. [Almost 800 names.]

___B. S. Wolfe, INDEX TO REVOLUTIONARY SOLDIERS OF IN AND OTHER PATRIOTS, Ye Olde Genealogie Shoppe, Indianapolis, IN, 1983.

Information regarding Revolutionary War participants who went into IA will be found in:

___M. H. S. Johnston, DAUGHTERS OF THE DAR [IOWA], 1897-1911, DAR of IA, Des Moines, IA, 1911.

___REVOLUTIONARY WAR SOLDIERS AND PATRIOTS BURIED IN IA, Walsworth Publishing Co., Marceline, MO, 1978.

8. KY through OH

For the state of <u>KY</u>, these works may turn out to be useful:

___J. H. S. Ardery, KY RECORDS, Genealogical Publishing Co., Baltimore, MD, 1926. [Estates and inventories of Revolutionary soldiers.]

___A. W. B. Bell, REVOLUTIONARY WAR SOLDIERS WHO SETTLED AND LIVED IN KY, several typewritten volumes, 1935-.

___A. W. Burns, ABSTRACTS OF PENSION PAPERS OF SOLDIERS OF THE REVOLUTIONARY, 1812, AND INDIAN WARS WHO SETTLED IN KY, Washington, DC, 1935-, over 20 volumes.

___C. C. Davis, REVOLUTION ANCESTORS OF KY DAR, DAR of KY, Frankfort, KY, 1928.

___M. H. Harding, compiler, GEORGE ROGERS CLARK AND HIS MEN, MILITARY RECORDS, 1778-1784, KY Historical Society, Frankfort, KY, 1981.

___W. R. Jillson, THE KY LAND GRANTS: A SYSTEMATIC INDEX TO ALL OF THE LAND GRANTS RECORDED IN THE STATE LAND OFFICE AT FRANKFORT, KY, 1782-1924, Filson Club Publication, No. 33, Louisville, KY, 1925.

___W. R. Jillson, OLD KY ENTRIES AND DEEDS, Filson Club Publication No. 35, Louisville, KY, 1925.

___K. G. Lindsay, KY'S REVOLUTIONARY WAR PENSIONERS, Kenma Publishing Co., Evansville, IN, 1977.

___E. W. McAdams, KY PIONEER AND COURT RECORDS, Genealogical Publshing Co., Baltimore, MD, 1967. [A roll of Revolutionary pensioners is included.]

___L. K. McGhee, PENSION ABSTRACTS OF MD SOLDIERS OF THE REVOLUTIONARY, 1812, AND INDIAN WARS WHO SETTLED IN KY, Washington, DC, no date.

___A. C. Quisenberry, REVOLUTIONARY SOLDIERS IN KY, Genealogical Printing Co., Baltimore, MD, 1974. [Nearly 3000 names.]

___S. M. Wilson, YEAR BOOK OF THE SOCIETY, SONS OF THE AMERICAN REVOLUTION IN THE COMMONWEALTH OF KY, The Society, Lexingon, KY, 1913. [Over 3500 names.]

___See this chapter, section 5, under VA, since the KY area was VA during the War.

In <u>LA</u>, some important volumes are:

___E. R. Churchill, compiler, SOLDIERS OF THE AMERICAN REVOLUTION UNDER BERNARDO DE GALVEZ, Library of Congress, Washington, DC.

___W. DeVille, LA SOLDIERS IN THE AMERICAN REVOLUTION, Smith Books, Ville Platte, LA, 1991.

___E. S. Mills, NATCHITOCHES COLONIALS: CENSUSES, MILITARY ROLLS, AND TAX LISTS, 1722-1803, Cane River Creole Series, Mills Historical Press, Tuscaloosa. AL, 1981.

___A. J. Robichaux, comp., trans., ed. LA CENSUS AND MILITIA LISTS, 2 vols., The Author, Harvey, LA, 1973.

In <u>ME</u>, which was a part of MA during the Revolutionary War, some of the most important volumes are:

___DAR, ME REVOLUTIONARY SOLDIERS GRAVES, The Society, Augusta, ME, 1940.

___C. E. And S. G. Fisher, compilers, SOLDIERS, SAILORS, AND PATRIOTS OF THE REVOLUTIONARY WAR, ME, National Sons of the American Revolution, Louisville, KY, 1982.

___C. A. Flagg, AN ALPHABETICAL INDEX OF REVOLUTIONARY PENSIONERS LIVING IN ME, Genealogical Publishing Co., Baltimore, MD, 1967. [More than 3400 names.]

___C. J. House, NAMES OF SOLDIERS OF THE AMERICAN REVOLUTION WHO APPLIED FOR STATE BOUNTY, Genealogical Publishing Co., Baltimore, MD, 1967. [About 1000 names.]

___E. R. Houston, ME REVOLUTIONARY SOLDIERS' GRAVES, DAR of ME, Portland, ME, 1940.

___ME Sons of the American Revolution, ME AT VALLEY FORGE, Burleigh and Flint, Augusta, ME, 1910. [About 1000 names.]

___Mrs. P. T. Tate, ROSTER AND ANCESTRAL ROLL, DAR of ME, Farmington, ME, 1948. [1700 members and their ancestors.]

___VITAL STATISTICS COPIED FROM THE ME FARMER, 1832-52, University Microfilms, Ann Arbor, 1949, 3 volumes.

Three books listing Revolutionary War participants in <u>MI</u> are:

___J. C. Curry, MI REVOLUTIONARY WAR PENSION PAYMENTS, MI Heritage, volumes 1-2, 1959-60. [Just under 2000 names.]

___DAR, MI, HISTORICAL RECORD OF THE MI DAUGHTERS OF THE AMERICAN REVOLUTION, 1893-1952, 2 vols., Ann Arbor Press, Ann Arbor, MI, 1930-52.

___S. I. Silliman, MI MILITARY RECORDS, MI Historical Committee

Bulletin 12, Lansing, MI, 1920. [About 250 names.]

Volumes pertaining to <u>MS</u> include:
__J. E. S. King, MS COURT RECORDS, 1799-1835, Genealogical Publishing Co., Baltimore, MD, 1969. [About 75 men.]
__Mrs. W. R. Parkes, MS DAUGHTERS AND THEIR ANCESTORS, Starkville Publ., Starkville, MS 1965. [Over 3000 ancestors.]
__A. T. Welch, FAMILY RECORDS: MS REVOLUTIONARY SOLDIERS, Genealogical Publishing Co., Baltimore, MD, 1956. [Over 400 soldiers.]

There are also several books which list numerous veterans and their <u>MO</u> descendants:
__A. W. Burns, MO PENSION RECORDS OF SOLDIERS OF THE REVOLUTIONARY, 1812, AND INDIAN WARS, Washington, DC, 1937.
__DAR of MO, MO STATE DIRECTORY, The Society, Jefferson City, MO, latest issue.
__A. K. Houts and H. Eastman, REVOLUTIONARY SOLDIERS BURIED IN MO, The Author, Kansas City, MO, 1966. [About 1000 men.]
__L. K. McGhee, MO REVOLUTIONARY, 1812, AND INDIAN WAR SOLDIERS PENSION LIST, typescript, VA State Library, Richmond, VA, 1955.
__MO REVOLUTIONARY SOLDIERS AND THEIR DESCENDANTS, Jefferson City, MO.
__S. L. Pompey, A PARTIAL LIST OF VETERANS OF THE AMERICAN REVOLUTION, THE CIVIL WAR, AND THE SPANISH WAR BURIED IN MO, Johnson County Historical Society, Warrensburg, MO, 1962.

A volume dealing with <u>NM</u> descendants of Revolutionary War participants is:
__NM State DAR, NM DAR LINEAGE BOOK, The NM Society, Albuquerque, NM, 1972.

For <u>OH</u>, these works are among the better sources:
__G. M. Brumbaugh, REVOLUTIONARY WAR RECORDS: VA ARMY AND NAVY FORCES WITH BOUNTY LAND WARRANTS FOR VA MILITARY DISTRICT OF OH, Genealogical Publishing Co., Baltimore, MD, 1936. [About 7100 names.]

___Cincinnati Chapter, DAR, INDEX OF PATRIOTS, REVOLUTION-
ARY WAR HEROES, AND THEIR FAMILIES, The Chapter, Cincinnati, OH, 1983.

___J. D. Dailey, THE OFFICIAL ROSTER OF SOLDIERS OF THE
AMERICAN REVOLUTION WHO LIVED IN OH, DAR of OH,
Columbus, OH, 1938, volume 2.

___THE FIRELANDS PIONEER, Firelands Historical Society, Norwalk,
OH, 1858-78, 1882-1937, volumes 1-13, and new series volumes 1-25,
with INDEX, 1858-1927.

___F. O. Henderson, THE OFFICIAL ROSTER OF THE SOLDIERS
OF THE AMERICAN REVOLUTION BURIED IN OH, Heer
Printing, Columbus, OH, 1929-59, 3 volumes. [Over 7000 listings.]

___OH Sons of the American Revolution, REVOLUTIONARY
SOLDIERS BURIED IN OH, The Society, YEARBOOK, 1898, pp.
162-214, and 1900, pp. 89-94.

___See this chapter, section 5, under VA.

9. OK through WI

OK volumes which list veterans and their
descendants are:

___L. Spillers, A ROSTER OF THE OK
SOCIETY AND REGISTER OF
ANCESTORS, DAR of OK, Tulsa, OK, 1959.

___M. M. Willson, FIRST SUPPLEMENT TO A ROSTER OF THE OK
SOCIETY AND REGISTER OF ANCESTORS, DAR of OK, Tulsa,
OK, 1964.

For OR, this work can be looked into:
___L. W. Goodrich, ROSTER OF ANCESTORS, DAR of OR,
Tillamook, OR, 1963.

Investigations pertaining to Revolutionary War participants and
persons descended from them in the state of TN may be carried out by
consulting the books below. Many NC veterans were granted land in TN,
an area which was NC territory during the War.

___J. T. Acklen and others, TN RECORDS, Genealogical Publishing Co.,
Baltimore, MD, 1933, 2 volumes.

___P. J. Allen, TN SOLDIERS IN THE REVOLUTION, DAR of TN,
King, Bristol, TN, 1935. [Roster of soldiers in Washington and
Sullivan Counties, over 1500 men.]

___Z. Armstrong, SOME TN HEROES OF THE REVOLUTION,
Lookout Publishing, Chattanooga, TN, 1933-5.

___Z. Armstrong, TWENTY-FOUR HUNDRED TN PENSIONERS:

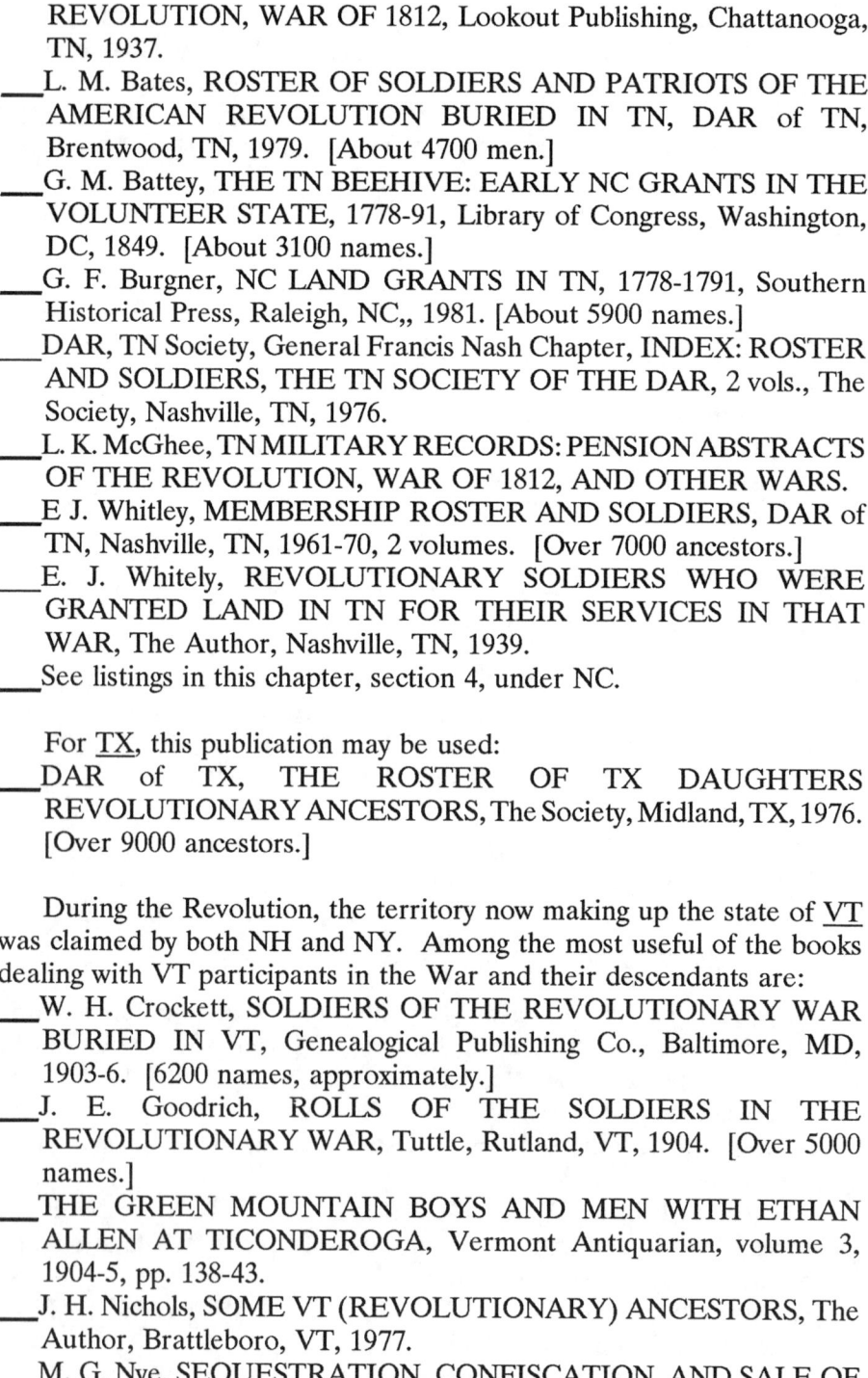

78

REVOLUTION, WAR OF 1812, Lookout Publishing, Chattanooga, TN, 1937.

___L. M. Bates, ROSTER OF SOLDIERS AND PATRIOTS OF THE AMERICAN REVOLUTION BURIED IN TN, DAR of TN, Brentwood, TN, 1979. [About 4700 men.]

___G. M. Battey, THE TN BEEHIVE: EARLY NC GRANTS IN THE VOLUNTEER STATE, 1778-91, Library of Congress, Washington, DC, 1849. [About 3100 names.]

___G. F. Burgner, NC LAND GRANTS IN TN, 1778-1791, Southern Historical Press, Raleigh, NC,, 1981. [About 5900 names.]

___DAR, TN Society, General Francis Nash Chapter, INDEX: ROSTER AND SOLDIERS, THE TN SOCIETY OF THE DAR, 2 vols., The Society, Nashville, TN, 1976.

___L. K. McGhee, TN MILITARY RECORDS: PENSION ABSTRACTS OF THE REVOLUTION, WAR OF 1812, AND OTHER WARS.

___E J. Whitley, MEMBERSHIP ROSTER AND SOLDIERS, DAR of TN, Nashville, TN, 1961-70, 2 volumes. [Over 7000 ancestors.]

___E. J. Whitely, REVOLUTIONARY SOLDIERS WHO WERE GRANTED LAND IN TN FOR THEIR SERVICES IN THAT WAR, The Author, Nashville, TN, 1939.

___See listings in this chapter, section 4, under NC.

For TX, this publication may be used:

___DAR of TX, THE ROSTER OF TX DAUGHTERS REVOLUTIONARY ANCESTORS, The Society, Midland, TX, 1976. [Over 9000 ancestors.]

During the Revolution, the territory now making up the state of VT was claimed by both NH and NY. Among the most useful of the books dealing with VT participants in the War and their descendants are:

___W. H. Crockett, SOLDIERS OF THE REVOLUTIONARY WAR BURIED IN VT, Genealogical Publishing Co., Baltimore, MD, 1903-6. [6200 names, approximately.]

___J. E. Goodrich, ROLLS OF THE SOLDIERS IN THE REVOLUTIONARY WAR, Tuttle, Rutland, VT, 1904. [Over 5000 names.]

___THE GREEN MOUNTAIN BOYS AND MEN WITH ETHAN ALLEN AT TICONDEROGA, Vermont Antiquarian, volume 3, 1904-5, pp. 138-43.

___J. H. Nichols, SOME VT (REVOLUTIONARY) ANCESTORS, The Author, Brattleboro, VT, 1977.

___M. G. Nye, SEQUESTRATION, CONFISCATION, AND SALE OF

ESTATES, State Papers of VT, 6th Volume, VT Secretary of State, Montpelier, VT, 1941.

For <u>WA</u>, look into:
___DAR of WA, HISTORY AND REGISTER, The Society, Seattle, WA, 1924-72, 3 volumes and Supplement.

<u>WV</u> veterans and those living in WV who have descended from Revolutionary War participants are listed in:
___R. B. Johnson, WEST VIRGINIANS IN THE AMERICAN REVOLUTION, WV Historical Society Publication 1, Parkersburg, WV, 1959. [Over 1300 biographies.]
___V. A. Lewis, THE SOLDIERY OF WV, Department of Archives and History, 3rd Biennial Report, News-Mail, Charleston, WV, 1910.
___E. P. Perkins, WV REVOLUTIONARY PENSIONS, 1935, volume 1.
___A. W. Reddy, WV REVOLUTIONARY ANCESTORS WHOSE SERVICES WERE NON-MILITARY, Genealogical Publishing Co., Baltimore, MD, 1930. [About 2000 men.]

Data relating to persons living in <u>WI</u> who have reported Revolutionary War ancestors will be found in:
___DAR of WI, ROSTER: REVOLUTIONARY WAR ANCESTORS, 1891-1964, The Society, Port Washington, WI, 1965.

Chapter 5

LOCAL SOURCES

▬▬▬▬▬▬▬ In addition to national and state sources of data on
1. Introduction Revolutionary War personnel, there are likely to be
at least some records at the city, village, town, and/or
▬▬▬▬▬▬▬ county levels. Among the possibilities are family
Bible records, cemetery records, gravestone
inscriptions, church records, city histories, town histories, county histories,
court records, genealogical periodical articles, local genealogical societies,
local historical societies, marriage anniversary accounts in newspapers,
mortuary records, newspaper accounts of battles, newspaper obituaries,
and published family genealogies. These and many other possible sources
of genealogical information on your Revolutionary War ancestor are
treated in detail with precise instructions for searching in this volume:
__Geo. K. Schweitzer, GENEALOGICAL SOURCE HANDBOOK, $15
postpaid from Geo. K. Schweitzer, at 407 Ascot Court, Knoxville, TN
37923-5807.

In the three sections to follow some of the better possibilities from
among the above local sources will be discussed in detail. It is important
to check the cities, towns, and counties where your ancestor lived when he
enlisted, where he lived after the war, and where he died and was buried.

▬▬▬▬▬▬▬ If you know the city, town, and/or county
2. Place of enlistment where your Revolutionary War veteran
enlisted, there are a number of searches you
▬▬▬▬▬▬▬ can make in order to find the records. The
first inquiry should take place within your
family to see if anyone knows of records which were kept in a family Bible
or prayer book. The most usual things recorded there were birth,
marriage, and death dates, but sometimes Revolutionary War enlistments
or service were recorded. You should also inquire to see if anyone in the
family knows of the existence of a family genealogical account which has
been published.

The second move that it will be profitable to make is to look in the
following volumes for published local records. These volumes give
materials relating to numerous counties in which participants of the war
lived before the war, lived after the war, or were buried.
__L. Horowitz, A BIBLIOGRAPHY OF MILITARY NAME LISTS

FROM PRE-1675 TO 1900; A GUIDE TO GENEALOGICAL
SOURCES, Scarecrow Press, Metuchen, NJ, 1990, pages 70-451.
___National Society, DAR, DAR LIBRARY CATALOG, VOLUME 2:
STATE AND LOCAL HISTORIES AND RECORDS, The Society,
Washington, DC, 1986.

The third approach you should make is to look for city, town, and/or
county history books, especially ones published within 60 years after the
Revolutionary War. These often carried details of military units raised in
their area along with rosters of men who served from the locality. To find
such histories, consult:
___M. J. Kaminkow, US LOCAL HISTORIES IN THE LIBRARY OF
CONGRESS, Magna Carta, Baltimore, MD, 1975, 5 volumes.
Once you have located pertinent volumes, you may have them borrowed
for you through interlibrary loan at your local library.

Then, fourthly, you can dispatch an SASE to the city clerk, the town
clerk, and/or the county court clerk to ask if any Revolutionary War
enlistee records were kept. The addresses of many of these clerks may be
obtained from:
___E. P. Bentley, COUNTY COURTHOUSE BOOK, Genealogical
Publishing Co., Baltimore, MD, latest edition.

As a fifth action to take, letters of inquiry along with SASEs should be
addressed to the local genealogical society, the local historical society, and
the local library. Your inquiries to the genealogical and historical societies
should ask about any Revolutionary War records giving enlistees and/or
local military unit histories. Addresses of local genealogical societies may
be obtained from:
___E. P. Bentley, THE GENEALOGISTS ADDRESS BOOK,
Genealogical Publishing Co., Baltimore, MD, latest edition.
___V. N. Chambers, editor, THE GENEALOGICAL HELPER, Everton
Publishers, Logan, UT, latest July-August issue.
Addresses of local historical societies will be found in the volume just
mentioned by Bentley and in:
___DIRECTORY: HISTORICAL SOCIETIES AND AGENCIES IN
THE US AND CANADA, Nashville, TN, latest edition.
Your letter and SASE to the local library should ask about local histories,
church records, and newspapers published during and after the war.
Addresses of local libraries are obtainable in:
___AMERICAN LIBRARY DIRECTORY, Bowker, New York, NY,
latest issue.

A <u>sixth</u> approach that often pans out is another quest for newspaper information. You should see if the following volumes list any local newspapers for the local area of your interest during the war years.

___C. S. Brigham, HISTORY AND BIBLIOGRAPHY OF AMERICAN NEWSPAPERS, 1690-1820, American Antiquarian Society, Worcester, MA, 1961, 2 volumes. See also the supplement published in Proceedings of the American Antiquarian Society <u>72</u>(1971)15-62.

___NEWSPAPERS IN MICROFILM, US Library of Congress, Washington, DC, 1973; SUPPLEMENT, 1978.

___A CHECKLIST OF AMERICAN 18TH CENTURY NEWSPAPERS IN THE LIBRARY OF CONGRESS, The Library, Washington, DC, 1936.

Should you discover newspapers which appear promising, the volumes above give you information regarding where they may be obtained.

---

3. Place of residence

With a knowledge of the city, town, and/or county (or cities, towns, and/or counties) in which your veteran lived after the War, you can pursue your search even further. Again, as a <u>first</u> step, you should make another careful survey of your family to make sure you haven't missed a great aunt or some other of the oldest living members.

Following this, pursue the <u>second</u> line of inquiry by searching the book by Horowitz and the published DAR Catalog volume for published local records (section 2).

Then, in the same fashion as before (section 2), the <u>third</u> approach involves the search for city, town, and/ or county histories for the areas where your ancestor lived. Histories often carried biographical references or even sketches of citizens, and often Revolutionary War service will be mentioned, sometimes considerable detail being given. The works by Kaminkow (section 2) should be consulted, and, if you locate suitable volumes, your local library can probably borrow them on interlibrary loan.

The <u>fourth</u> action to take is the sending of inquiries (including SASEs) to local court clerks, local historical societies, local genealogical societies, and local libraries asking about Revolutionary War records, especially: (a) lists of resident veterans, (b) newspaper accounts of marriage anniversaries of your veteran, (c) records of Revolutionary War organizations to which your ancestor or his descendants may have belonged, and (d) local histories which are available. The procedures for obtaining addresses to which you should write have been explained in section 2, this chapter.

A _fifth_ thing to do is to carry out the search for appropriate newspapers by using the three reference volumes given in paragraph 5, section 2, of this chapter.

■■■■■■■■■■■■■ Knowing the place and exact or approximate date
4. Place of death of death of your Revolutionary War veteran, there
are numerous routes of exploration you need to
■■■■■■■■■■■■■ take for information concerning him. _First_, check
with your family concerning the existence of family
Bible or prayer book records. It is possible that your ancestor's death date
in the record may carry a notation or even some detail about military service.

Second, address an inquiry accompanied by an SASE and a check for
$4 to the caretaker of the cemetery in which your ancestor is buried. Ask
if there are any detailed records on those who have been buried there, and
if so, whether there is anything about your ancestor's Revolutionary War
record. If you have not seen the gravestone, also ask for a copy or a
picture of the inscription, since these inscriptions often carried notations
on military service.

Third, address letters of inquiry accompanied by SASE's to the local
court clerk, local library, local genealogical society, and local historical
society. Ask them about several things: (a) whether there are local burial
or death records which might mention Revolutionary War service, (b)
whether existing mortuaries might still have records of previous mortuaries
which could have handled the burial, (c) whether there are local church
records which might have burial data in them, (d) whether there might be
a newspaper obituary, (e) whether there are city, town, or county histories
which might give Revolutionary War soldier biographies, and (f) whether
there might have been a patriotic organization which took part in the
funeral service and kept a record of it. Addresses for libraries and
societies will be found in the volumes mentioned in section 2 of this
chapter.

Fourth, be sure to check the following set of books for local histories
which might give Revolutionary War veteran data or published lists of
veterans burials:
__M. J. Kaminkow, US LOCAL HISTORIES IN THE LIBRARY OF
CONGRESS, Magna Carta, Baltimore, MD, 1975, 5 volumes.

__P. W. Filby, BIBLIOGRAPHY OF COUNTY HISTORIES IN AMERICA, Genealogical Publishing Co., Baltimore, MD, 1985.

__L. Horowitz, A BIBLIOGRAPHY OF MILITARY NAME LISTS FROM PRE-1675 TO 1900; A GUIDE TO GENEALOGICAL SOURCES, Scarecrow Press, Metuchen, NJ, 1990, pages 70-451.

__National Society, DAR, DAR LIBRARY CATALOG, VOLUME 2: STATE AND LOCAL HISTORIES AND RECORDS, The Society, Washington, DC, 1986.

Finally, don't overlook a newspaper search using the volumes listed in item 5 of section 2 of this chapter.

Chapter 6

HISTORIES: INDIVIDUAL, REGIMENTAL, BATTLE, STATE, GROUP

███████████████
1. Introduction
███████████████

Once you have identified your veteran, discovered his state, and found his regiment or ship, you are then in position to trace him through his wartime experiences. This can be done by seeking documents written by individuals in his military unit, writings giving a detailed history of his regiment, books dedicated to descriptions of particular battles, volumes chronicling the War as fought by the forces from individual states, histories of special groups, histories of the Continental army, British histories of the War, and appropriate maps of various operations of the army and navy. There is a good possibility that you can get a fairly detailed view of your ancestor's military career through the use of volumes of the type mentioned in this chapter.

███████████████
2. Individual histories
███████████████

During the Revolution, many participants kept diaries, journals, or travel accounts. Quite a sizable number also wrote letters or had letters written for them if they were illiterate. A notable number of these have survived and are scattered in various special library collections and manuscript repositories. Further, a number of veterans after the War wrote memoirs, personal recollections, and autobiographies. Many biographies were also written, especially on officers.

Unfortunately, locating these valuable documents is usually not easy. To attempt to find them you need to write to the archives and libraries of the state under which your ancestor served (see sections 4 and 6, Chapter 2, for addresses). Be sure to examine the pertinent archives guides which are listed in the latter half of section 6, Chapter 2. In addition, many available sources of biographical data are listed in the following bibliographic works:

___J. T. White and C. H. Lesser, FIGHTERS FOR INDEPENDENCE, University of Chicago Press, Chicago, IL, 1977, pp. 22-109.

___J. Shy, THE AMERICAN REVOLUTION: A BIBLIOGRAPHY, AHM Publishing Corp., Northbrook, IL, 1973, pp. 62-77.

___W. Mathew, AMERICAN DIARIES: BIBLIOGRAPHY OF AMERICAN DIARIES WRITTEN PRIOR TO 1861, University of CA Press, Berkeley, CA, 1945.

___W. Mathew, AMERICAN DIARIES IN MANUSCRIPT, 1580-1954: A DESCRIPTIVE BIBLIOGRAPHY, University of GA Press, Athens, GA, 1974.

___H. M. Forbes, NEW ENGLAND DIARIES, 1620-1800: A DESCRIPTIVE CATALOG, The Author, Topfield, MA, 1923.

___D. L. Smith, ERA OF THE AMERICAN REVOLUTION: A BIBLIOGRAPHY, ABC-Clio, Santa Barbara, CA, 1975.

___R. W. Coakley and S. Conn, THE WAR OF THE AMERICAN REVOLUTION: NARRATIVE, CHRONOLOGY, AND BIBLIOGRAPHY, Center of Military History, US Army, Washington, DC, 1975.

___A. M. Case, BIBLIOGRAPHIC INDEX, Wilson, New York, NY, each year. [Look under UNITED STATES - History - Revolution.]

Two overall general reference works to leaders in the Revolution which will be helpful for short outlinetype biographies is:

___J. Krail, WHO WAS WHO DURING THE AMERICAN REVOLUTION, Bobbs-Merrill, Indianapolis, IN, 1976.

___WHO WAS WHO IN AMERICAN HISTORY - THE MILITARY, Marquis, Chicago, IL, 1975.

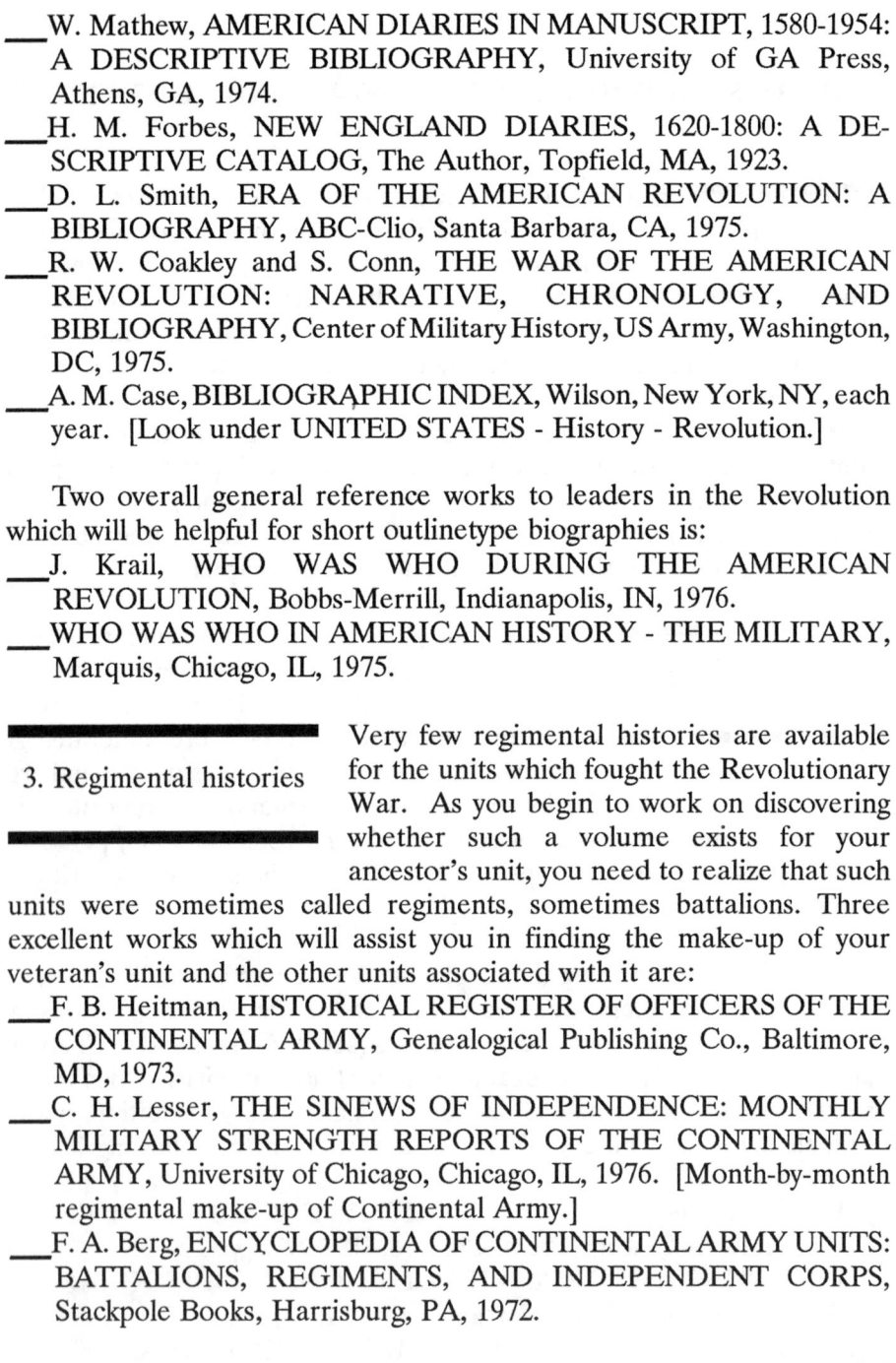

3. Regimental histories

Very few regimental histories are available for the units which fought the Revolutionary War. As you begin to work on discovering whether such a volume exists for your ancestor's unit, you need to realize that such units were sometimes called regiments, sometimes battalions. Three excellent works which will assist you in finding the make-up of your veteran's unit and the other units associated with it are:

___F. B. Heitman, HISTORICAL REGISTER OF OFFICERS OF THE CONTINENTAL ARMY, Genealogical Publishing Co., Baltimore, MD, 1973.

___C. H. Lesser, THE SINEWS OF INDEPENDENCE: MONTHLY MILITARY STRENGTH REPORTS OF THE CONTINENTAL ARMY, University of Chicago, Chicago, IL, 1976. [Month-by-month regimental make-up of Continental Army.]

___F. A. Berg, ENCYCLOPEDIA OF CONTINENTAL ARMY UNITS: BATTALIONS, REGIMENTS, AND INDEPENDENT CORPS, Stackpole Books, Harrisburg, PA, 1972.

Among the books and articles which either give regimental histories or list sources of such information are:

___J. B. Linn and W. Egle, PA IN THE WAR OF THE REVOLUTION, BATTALIONS AND LINE, 1775-83, Hart, Harrisburg, PA, 1880.

___A. H. Clark, A COMPLETE ROSTER OF COL. DAVID WATERBURY'S REGIMENT [DEFENSE OF NY CITY], Clark, New York, NY, 1897.

___E. M. Sanchez-Saavedra, A GUIDE TO VA MILITARY ORGANIZATIONS IN THE AMERICAN REVOLUTION, VA State Library, Richmond, VA, 1978.

___C. L. Ward, THE DE CONTINENTALS, Historical Society of DE, Wilmington, DE, 1941.

___C. A. Flagg and W. O. Waters, VA'S SOLDIERS IN THE REVOLUTION: A BIBLIOGRAPHY OF MUSTER AND PAY ROLLS AND REGIMENTAL HISTORIES, VA Magazine of History and Biography, volume 19, pp. 402-14, volume 20, pp. 52-68, 181-94,267-81, volume 21, pp. 337-46, volume 22, pp. 57-67, 171-86.

___J. B. B. Trussell, Jr., THE PA LINE: REGIMENTAL ORGANIZATION AND OPERATIONS, PA Historical and Museum Commission, Harrisburg, PA, 1977.

___J. T. McAllister, VA MILITIA IN THE REVOLUTIONARY WAR, McAllister, Hot Springs, VA, 1913.

___H. F. Rankin, THE NC CONTINENTALS, University of NC Press, Chapel Hill, NC, 1971.

___R. Steuart, A HISTORY OF THE MD LINE IN THE REVOLUTIONARY WAR, Society of the Cincinnati of MD, Towson, MD, 1969.

___C. P. Bennett, THE DELAWARE REGIMENT IN THE REVOLUTION in PA Magazine of History, volume 9 (1885) 455.

___G. A. Billias, GENERAL JOHN GLOVER AND HIS MARBLEHEAD MARINERS, Holt, New York, NY, 1960.

___P. F. Copeland and M. Zlatich, 2ND VA REGIMENT in Military Collector and Historian, volume 17 (1965) 86.

___A. B. Gardner, THE NY CONTINENTAL LINE in Magazine of American History, volume 7 (1881) 401.

___N. Goold, COL. JAMES SCAMMANS 30TH REGIMENT OF FOOT, ME Historical Society Collections, 2nd Series, volume 10 (1899) 337.

___N. Goold, COL. EDMUND PHINNEY'S 18TH CONTINENTAL REGIMENT, ME Historical Society Collections, 2nd Series, volume 10 (1899) 45.

___F. Kidder, HISTORY OF THE 1ST NH REGIMENT, Genealogical Publishing Co., Baltimore, MD, 1868.

___O. A. Roberts, HISTORY OF THE MILITARY COMPANY OF

MA, Mudge & Son, Boston, MA, 1895-1901, 4 volumes.
___W. S. Stryker, THE NJ CONTINENTAL LINE IN THE VA CAM-
PAIGN OF 1781, Murphy, Trenton, NJ, 1882.
___L. G. Tyler, THE OLD VA LINE IN THE MIDDLE STATES,
Tyler's Quarterly, volume 12 (Jul-Oct, 1930) 1, 90.
___A. J. Alexander, PA'S REVOLUTIONARY MILITIA, PA Magazine
of History and Biography, volume 69 (Jan, 1945) 15.
___J. R. Anderson, MILITIA LAW IN REVOLUTIONARY NJ, NJ
Historical Society Proceedings, new series, volume 76 (Oct, 1958) 280
and volume 77 (Jan, 1959).
___L. L. Gobbel, THE MILITIA IN NC, Trinity College Historical
Society Papers, volume 13 (1919) 35.
___R. C. Pugh, THE REVOLUTIONARY MILITIA IN THE
SOUTHERN CAMPAIGN, William and Mary Quarterly, 3rd series,
volume 14 (1957) 154.
___CT Historical Society, ORDERLY BOOKS AND JOURNALS KEPT
BY CT MEN, The Society, Hartfort, CT, 1899.

Another approach to the history of a regiment is to seek biographical
materials by or on its officers (see the previous section). State histories
and battle histories can often be of value. These will be discussed in
succeeding sections. Still a further way to obtain data on a regiment's
history is to look for orderly books. Orderly books were books of records
kept by Revolutionary War officers in which they recorded instructions
and orders which came down from superior officers. Some contain only
orders; others have a log of the military unit's activities. The best sources
for orderly books are the Library of Congress (about 90), the National
Archives (about 70), The Huntington Library, state archives, state
historical societies, and state libraries, although a few may be found in
local libraries and museums.

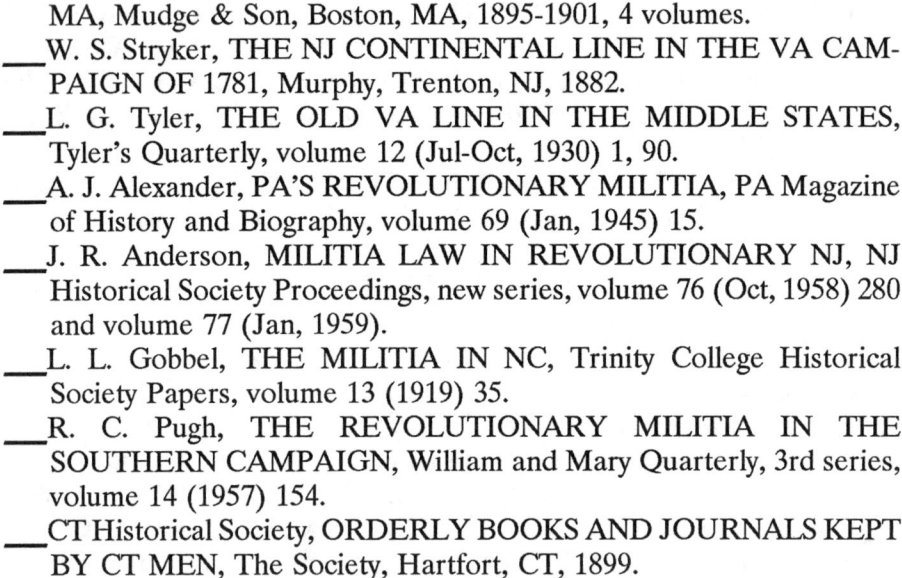

4. Battle histories

Once you discover which battles your ancestor's
regiment participated in, you may be interested to
read about the military action in detail. It is often
possible to pinpoint the exact places in which your
veterans's unit fought during various phases of the
battle. Your first approach should be to use a very good volume which
contains short accounts of the major battles plus further references:
___M. M. Boatner, III, ENCYCLOPEDIA OF THE AMERICAN
REVOLUTION, McKay, New York, NY, 1966.
Data on the various battles, the units which fought in them, and the
number of casualties are contained in:

___H. H. Peckham, THE TOLL OF INDEPENDENCE, University of Chicago Press, Chicago, IL, 1974.

You may then proceed, if you wish, to more detailed studies of the battles. Listed below are some of the better volumes dealing with individual battles. At least one volume is given for each major battle, the volumes being listed in the chronological order in which the battles occurred. At the beginning of the list are three general overall volumes, and at the end of the list are a couple of books treating the action on the frontier. Please recognize that this list is not complete; it is only meant to help get you started. There are numerous other works which librarians in larger libraries can assist you to find.

___H. B. Carrington, BATTLES OF THE AMERICAN REVOLUTION, Barnes, New York, NY, 1881.

___J. B. Mitchell, DECISIVE BATTLES OF THE AMERICAN REVOLUTION, Fawcett, New York, NY, 1962.

___H. B. Dawson, BATTLES OF THE US BY SEA AND LAND, Johnson, Fry, New York, NY, 1858.

___A. French, DAY OF LEXINGTON AND CONCORD, Reprint, Spartanburg, SC, 1969.

___R. Frothingham, HISTORY OF THE SIEGE OF BOSTON, Little and Brown, Boston, MA, 1851.

___R. Ketchum, DECISIVE DAY: THE BATTLE FOR BUNKER HILL, Doubleday, Garden City, NY, 1974.

___J. R. Elting, THE BATTLE OF BUNKER'S HILL, Freneau Press, Monmouth Beach, NY, 1975.

___H. Bird, ATTACK ON QUEBEC, Oxford University Press, New York, NY, 1968.

___R. M. Hatch, THRUST FOR CANADA, Houghton Mifflin, Boston, MA, 1979.

___H. F. Rankin, THE MOORE'S CREEK BRIDGE CAMPAIGN, NC Historical Review, volume 30, 1953, pp. 23-60.

___E. I. Manders, THE BATTLE OF LONG ISLAND, Freneau Press, Monmouth Beach, NJ, 1978.

___B. Bliven, BATTLE FOR MANHATTAN, Holt, New York, NY, 1956.

___H. P. Johnston, CAMPAIGN OF 1776 AROUND NY AND BROOKLYN, Long Island Historical Society, Brooklyn, NY, 1876.

___H. P. Johnston, BATTLE OF HARLEM HEIGHTS, Macmillan, New York, NY, 1897.

___A. H. Bill, THE CAMPAIGN OF PRINCETON, Princeton University Press, Princeton, NY, 1948.

___A. A. Merrill, BATTLE OF WHITE PLAINS, Analysis, Chappaqua,

NY, 1976.

___S. S. Smith, THE BATTLE OF PRINCETON, Freneau, Monmouth Beach, NJ, 1967.

___S. S. Smith, THE BATTLE OF TRENTON, Freneau, Monmouth Beach, NJ, 1965.

___S. S. Smith, FIGHT FOR THE DELAWARE 1777, Freneau Press, Monmouth Beach, NJ, 1970.

___S. S. Smith, THE BATTLE OF BRANDYWINE, Freneau Press, Monmouth Beach, NJ, 1976.

___H. Bird, MARCH TO SARATOGA, Oxford University Press, New York, NY, 1963.

___R. Furneaux, THE BATTLE OF SARATOGA, Stein and Day, New York, NY, 1971.

___J. R. Elting, THE BATTLES OF SARATOGA, Freneau Press, Monmouth Beach, NJ, 1977.

___H. Hall, BATTLE OF BENNINGTON, Library of Congress, Washington, DC, 1826.

___A. H. Bill, VALLEY FORGE, Harper, New York, NY, 1952.

___S. S. Smith, THE BATTLE OF MONMOUTH, Freneau, Monmouth Beach, NJ, 1964.

___A. A. Lawrence, STORM OVER SAVANNAH: THE SIEGE IN 1779, University of GA Press, Athens, GA, 1951.

___H. P. Johnston, STORMING OF STONY POINT, DeCapo, New York, NY, 1900.

___A. T. Norton, HISTORY OF SULLIVAN'S CAMPAIGN, The Author, Lima, NY, 1879.

___B. Tarleton, HISTORY OF THE CAMPAIGNS, 1780-1, Arno, New York, NY, 1787.

___R. F. Weigley, THE PARTISAN WAR: THE SC CAMPAIGN OF 1780-2, University of SC Press, Columbia, SC, 1970.

___G. S. McCowen, Jr., THE BRITISH OCCUPATION OF CHARLES-TON, University of SC Press, Columbia, SC, 1972.

___L. C. Draper, KING'S MOUNTAIN AND ITS HEROES, Thomson, Cincinnati, OH, 1881.

___B. Davis, THE COWPENS-GUILFORD COURT HOUSE CAMPAIGN, Lippincott, Philadelphia, PA, 1962.

___M. F. Treacy, PRELUDE TO YORKTOWN, University of NC Press, Chapel Hill, NC, 1881.

___H. P. Johnston, THE YORKTOWN CAMPAIGN, University of NC Press, Chapel Hill, NC, 1881.

___T. J. Fleming, BEAT THE LAST DRUM, St. Martin's Press, New York, NY, 1963.

___J. M. Sosin, THE REVOLUTIONARY FRONTIER, Holt, Rinehart, and Winston, New York, NY, 1967.

___D. Van Every, A COMPANY OF HEROES: THE AMERICAN FRONTIER, 1775-83, Morrow, New York, NY, 1962.

___K. W. Seineke, THE GEORGE ROGERS CLARK ADVENTURE IN IL, Polyanthos, New Orleans, LA, 1982.

Other books and some periodical articles describing battles are listed in:

___J. Shy, THE AMERICAN REVOLUTION: A BIBLIOGRAPHY, AHM Publishing Corporation, Northbrook, Il, 1973.

___R. W. Coakley and S. Conn, THE WAR OF THE AMERICAN REVOLUTION: NARRATIVE, CHRONOLOGY, AND BIBLIOGRAPHY, Center of Military History, US Army, Washington, DC, 1975.

___A. M. Case, BIBLIOGRAPHIC INDEX: A CUMULATIVE BIBLIOGRAPHY OF BIBLIOGRAPHIES, Wilson, New York, NY, each year. [Look under UNITED STATES - History - Revolution.]

___SUBJECT GUIDE TO BOOKS IN PRINT, Bowker, New York, NY, latest edition. [Look under names of battles.]

Data on the various battles, the units which fought in them, and the number of casualties are contained in:

___H. H. Peckham, THE TOLL OF INDEPENDENCE, University of Chicago Press, Chicago, IL, 1974.

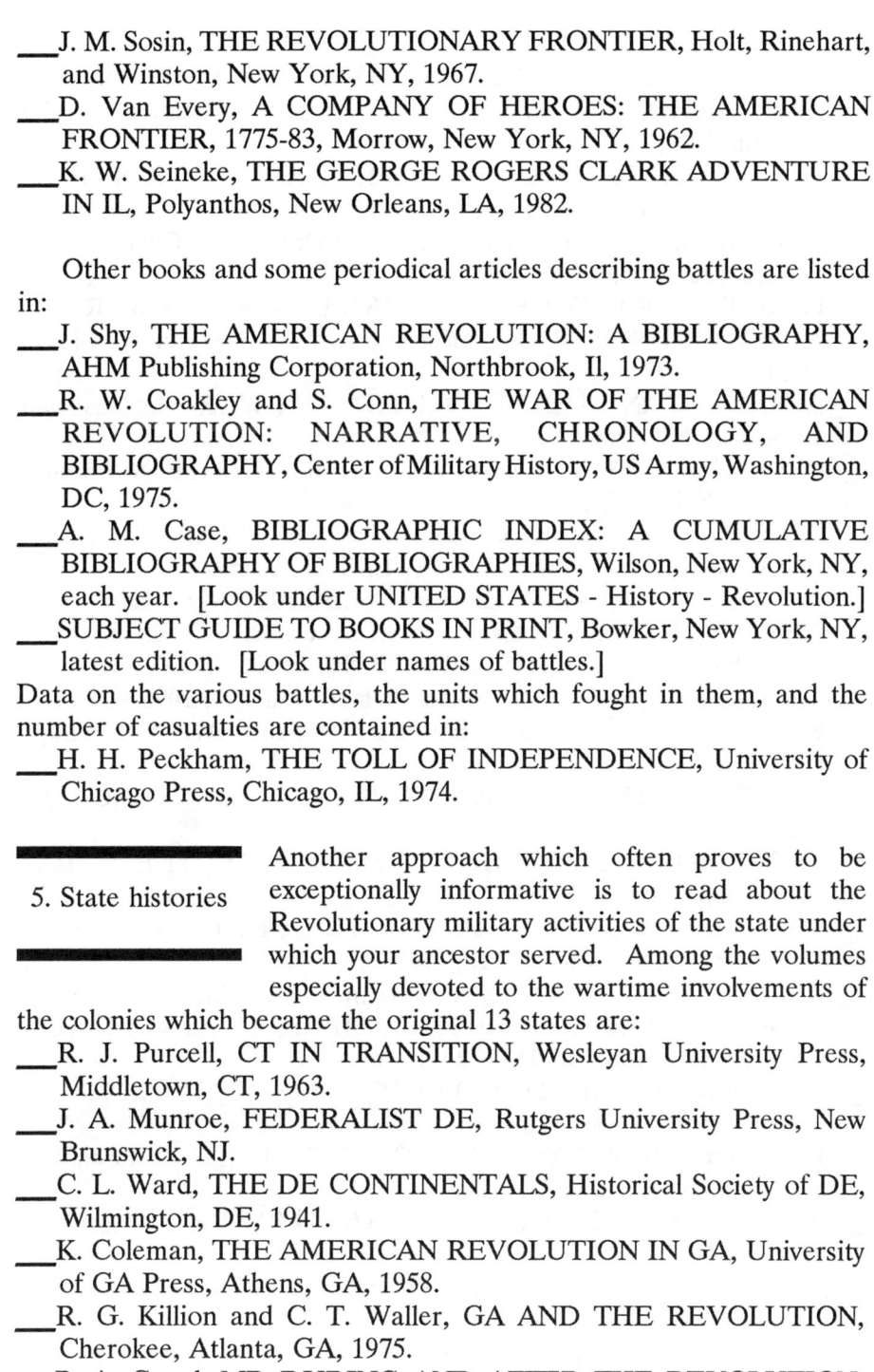

5. State histories Another approach which often proves to be exceptionally informative is to read about the Revolutionary military activities of the state under which your ancestor served. Among the volumes especially devoted to the wartime involvements of the colonies which became the original 13 states are:

___R. J. Purcell, CT IN TRANSITION, Wesleyan University Press, Middletown, CT, 1963.

___J. A. Munroe, FEDERALIST DE, Rutgers University Press, New Brunswick, NJ.

___C. L. Ward, THE DE CONTINENTALS, Historical Society of DE, Wilmington, DE, 1941.

___K. Coleman, THE AMERICAN REVOLUTION IN GA, University of GA Press, Athens, GA, 1958.

___R. G. Killion and C. T. Waller, GA AND THE REVOLUTION, Cherokee, Atlanta, GA, 1975.

___P. A. Crowl, MD DURING AND AFTER THE REVOLUTION,

Hamden, CT, 1964.

___R. Stewart, A HISTORY OF THE MD LINE IN THE REVOLUTIONARY WAR, Society of the Cincinnati of MD, Towson, MD, 1969.

___R. J. Taylor, WESTERN MA IN THE REVOLUTION, Brown University Press, Providence, RI, 1954.

___R. F. Upton, REVOLUTIONARY NH, Dartmouth College Publications, Hanover, NH, 1936.

___L. Lundin, COCKPIT OF THE REVOLUTION: THE WAR FOR INDEPENDENCE IN NJ, Princeton University Press, Princeton, NJ, 1940.

___A. H. Bill, NJ AND THE REVOLUTIONARY WAR, Van Nostrand, Princeton, NJ, 1964.

___W. C. Abbott, NEW YORK CITY IN THE REVOLUTION, Scribner, New York, NY, 1929.

___T. Jones, HISTORY OF NY DURING THE REVOLUTIONARY WAR, Arno Press, New York, NY, 1879, 2 volumes.

___H. Fish, NY STATE: BATTLEGROUND OF THE REVOLUTIONARY WAR, Vantage, New York, NY, 1976.

___C. L. Davis, A BRIEF HISTORY OF NC TROOPS IN THE WAR OF THE REVOLUTION, Bellas, Philadelphia, PA, 1896.

___P. Russell, NC IN THE REVOLUTIONARY WAR, Heritage, Charlotte, NC, 1965.

___H. F. Rankin, THE NC CONTINENTALS, University of NC Press, Chapel Hill, NC, 1971.

___F. G. Bates, RI AND THE FORMATION OF THE UNION, Macmillan, New York, NY, 1898.

___I. H. Polishook, 1774-1795: RI AND THE UNION, Northwestern University Press, Evanston, IL, 1969.

___B. Cowell, SPIRIT OF 76 IN RI, Wright, Boston, MA, 1850.

___J. Drayton, MEMOIRS OF THE AMERICAN REVOLUTION, Miller, Charleston, SC, 1821, 2 volumes.

___D. Ramsay, THE HISTORY OF THE REVOLUTION OF SC, Collins, Trenton, NJ, 1785, 2 volumes.

___E. McCrady, HISTORY OF SC IN THE REVOLUTION, Russell and Russell, New York, NY, 1969.

___W. G. Simms, SC IN THE REVOLUTIONARY WAR, Walker and James, Charleston, SC, 1853.

___H. J. Eckenrode, THE REVOLUTION IN VA, Archon, Hamden, CT, 1964.

___F. M. Hart, THE VALLEY OF VA IN THE REVOLUTION, University of NC Press, Chapel Hill, NC, 1942.

Helpful volumes for the frontier areas and for the territory now represented by the state of FL are:

___J. M. Sosin, THE REVOLUTIONARY FRONTIER, Rinehart and Winston, New York, NY, 1967.

___D. Van Every, A COMPANY OF HEROES: THE AMERICAN FRONTIER, 1775-83, Morrow, New York, NY, 1962.

___S. C. Williams, TN DURING THE REVOLUTIONARY WAR, TN Historical Commission, Nashville, TN, 1944-.

___J. L. Wright, FL IN THE AMERICAN REVOLUTION, University of FL Press, Gainesville, FL, 1975.

Other listings of state history works which contain material on the American Revolution may be found in the following bibliography:

___M. J. Kaminkow, US LOCAL HISTORIES IN THE LIBRARY OF CONGRESS, Magna Carta Book Co., Baltimore, MD, 1975, 5 volumes.

Revolutionary War materials relating to individual states of the original 13 will also be found in general state histories, some of those containing large sections on the War being:

___H. J. Bingham, HISTORY OF CT, Lewis Historical Publishing Co., New York, NY, 1962, 4 volumes.

___J. T. Scharf and others, HISTORY OF DE, Richards and Co., Philadelphia, PA, 1888, 2 volumes.

___W. G. Cooper, THE STORY OF GA, American Historical Society, New York, NY, 1938.

___J. McSherry, A HISTORY OF MD, 1634-1848, Murphy, Baltimore, MD, 1850.

___J. T. Scharf, HISTORY OF MD FROM EARLIEST TIMES, Everts, Philadelphia, PA, 1879, 3 volumes.

___A. B. Hart, COMMONWEALTH HISTORY OF MA, States History Co., New York, NY, 1927-30, 5 volumes.

___J. Belknap, THE HISTORY OF NH, Bradford and Read, Boston, MA, 1813, 3 volumes.

___F. B. Lee, NJ AS A COLONY AND AS A STATE, Publishing Society of NJ, New York, NY, 1902, 4 volumes.

___A. Flick, HISTORY OF THE STATE OF NY, Friedman, New York, NY, 1933-7, 10 volumes.

___R. P. McCormick, NY FROM COLONY TO STATE, Princeton University Press, Princeton, NJ, 1964.

___R. P. McCormick, NY FROM COLONY TO STATE, Princeton University Press, Princeton, NJ, 1964.

___R. D. Connor, HISTORY OF NC, Lewis Publishing Co., Chicago, IL,

1919, volume 1.

___P. S. Klein and A. Hoogenboom, A HISTORY OF PA, PA State University Press, University Park, PA, 1980.

___E. Field, STATE OF RI AND PROVIDENCE PLANTATION: A HISTORY, Mason, Boston, MA, 1902, 3 volumes.

___D. D. Wallace, THE HISTORY OF SC, American Historical Society, New York, NY, 1934, 4 volumes.

___L. G. Tyler, HISTORY OF VA: FEDERAL PERIOD, 1763-1861, American Historical Society, Chicago, IL, 1924, volume 2.

Works relating to the frontier areas include:

___M. J. Smith, A HISTORY OF ME, Falmouth, Portland, ME, 1949.

___C. W. Alvord, THE CENTENNIAL HISTORY OF IL, IL Centennial Commission, Springfield, IL, 1920, volume 1.

___R. E. Corlew, TN, A SHORT HISTORY, University of TN Press, Knoxville, TN, 1981.

Other volumes will be listed in the work by Kaminkow mentioned at the conclusion of the previous paragraph.

If you care to really press your investigation to its limits, you can take a look into the appropriate state historical bibliographies. These works list large numbers of state and local works on history, quite a few of them containing Revolutionary War information. Among the more useful ones on the 13 original states are:

___C. A. Flagg, REFERENCE LIST ON CT LOCAL HISTORY, University of NY, Albany, NY, 1900.

___R. E. Schnare, Jr., LOCAL HISTORICAL RESOURCES IN CT, CT League of Historical Societies, Darien, CT, 1975.

___H. C. and M. B. Reed, A BIBLIOGRAPHY OF DE THROUGH 1960, University of DE Press, Newark, DE, 1966.

___A. R. Rowland, A BIBLIOGRAPHY OF WRITINGS ON GA HISTORY, Archon Books, Hamden, CT, 1966.

___E. P. Passano, AN INDEX TO THE SOURCE RECORDS OF ME: GENEALOGICAL, BIOGRAPHICAL, HISTORICAL, Genealogical Publishing Co., Baltimore, MD, 1967.

___C. A. Flagg, A GUIDE TO MA LOCAL HISTORY, Salem Press, Salem, MA, 1907.

___J. D. Haskell, Jr., MA: A BIBLIOGRAPHY OF ITS HISTORY, Hall, Boston, MA, 1976.

___O. G. Hammond and J. Hanrahan, BIBLIOGRAPHIES OF NH, NH Publishing Co., Somersworth, NH, 1971.

___E. J. Hanrahan, HAMMOND'S CHECKLIST OF NH HISTORY, NH Publishing Co., Somersworth, NH, 1971.

___N. R. Burr, A NARRATIVE AND DESCRIPTIVE BIBLIOGRAPHY OF NJ, Van Nostrand, New York, NY, 1964.

___M. M. Klein, NY IN THE AMERICAN REVOLUTION: A BIBLIOGRAPHY, NY American Revolution Bicentennial Commission, Albany, NY, 1974.

___H. Nestler, A BIBLIOGRAPHY OF NY STATE COMMUNITIES, COUNTIES, TOWNS, & VILLAGES, Friedman, Washington, NY, 1968.

___H. T. Lefler, A GUIDE TO THE STUDY AND READING OF NC HISTORY, University of NC Press, Chapel Hill, NC, 1969.

___M. L. Thornton, A BIBLIOGRAPHY OF NC, 1589-1956, University of NC Press, Chapel Hill, NC, 1958.

___G. Stevenson, NC LOCAL HISTORY: A SELECT BIBLIOGRAPHY, Office of Archives and History, Raleigh, NC, 1972.

___N. B. Wilkinson and others, BIBLIOGRAPHY OF PA HISTORY, PA Historical and Museum Commission, Harrisburg, PA, 1957, plus SUPPLEMENTS, 1976-80.

___C. S. Brigham, LIST OF BOOKS ON RI HISTORY, RI State Department of Education, Providence, RI, 1908.

___J. R. Bartlett, BIBLIOGRAPHY OF RI, Anthony, Providence, RI, 1864.

___J. H. Easterby, GUIDE TO THE STUDY AND READING OF SC HISTORY: A GENERAL CLASSIFIED BIBLIOGRAPHY, Reprint Co., Spartanburg, SC, 1975.

___J. R. Turnbull, BIBLIOGRAPHY OF SC, University of VA Press, Charlottesville, VA, 1956, 5 volumes.

___E. G. Swem, A BIBLIOGRAPHY OF VA, Bulletin of the VA State Library, volume 8, 1915, pp. 35-767.

___VA State Library, A BIBLIOGRAPHY OF VA, The Library, Richmond, VA, 1916-55, 5 volumes.

___R. O. Hummel, Jr., VA LOCAL HISTORY: A BIBLIOGRAPHY, VA State Library, Richmond, VA, 1976.

Bibliographies on VT and ME may also prove helpful for the military actions that occurred in them and for the soldiers and sailors these areas contributed to the conflict.

___M. D. Gilman, THE BIBLIOGRAPHY OF VT, Free Press, Burlington, VT, 1897.

___J. Williamson, BIBLIOGRAPHY OF ME, Thurston, Portland, ME, 1896, 2 volumes.

___Bangor Public Library, BIBLIOGRAPHY OF THE STATE OF ME, Hall, Boston, MA, 1962.

___J. E. Frost, ME GENEALOGY: A BIBLIOGRAPHICAL GUIDE,

ME Historical Society, Portland, ME, 1977.

6. Group histories

In your Revolutionary War investigations you may discover that your ancestor was a member of or was closely related to one of the special groups of participants in the hostilities. This could lead to your desire to know more of his circumstances and to understand the situation in which he was involved. There are numerous works which are very helpful for such purposes. Histories particularly devoted to the <u>French</u> in the war include:

___L. B. Kennett, THE FRENCH FORCES IN AMERICA, Greenwood, Westport, CT, 1977.

___T. W. Balch, THE FRENCH IN AMERICA DURING THE WAR OF INDEPENDENCE, Porter and Coates, Philadelphia, PA, 1891-5, 2 volumes.

___J. Merlant, SOLDIERS AND SAILORS OF FRANCE IN THE AMERICAN WAR OF INDEPENDENCE, Scribner, New York, NY, 1920.

___S. Bousal, WHEN THE FRENCH WERE HERE, Doubleday, Doran, Garden City, NY, 1945.

___E. M. Stone, OUR FRENCH ALLIES, Providence Press, Providence, RI, 1884.

___J. B. Perkins, FRANCE IN THE AMERICAN REVOLUTION, Corner House, Williamstown, MA, 1911.

___J. B. Perkins, FRANCE IN THE AMERICAN REVOLUTION, Franklin, New York, NY, 1970.

Works which go into great detail regarding <u>Loyalists</u> are:

___M. B. Norton, THE BRITISH-AMERICANS: LOYALIST EXILES IN ENGLAND, 1774-89, Little, Brown, Boston, MA, 1972.

___N. Callahan, ROYAL RAIDERS: THE TORIES OF THE AMERICAN REVOLUTION, Bobbs-Merrill, Indianapolis, IN, 1963. [No lists.]

___D. B. Chidsey, THE LOYALISTS: THE STORY OF THOSE AMERICANS WHO FOUGHT AGAINST INDEPENDENCE, Crown, New York, NY, 1973.

___A. E. Ryerson, THE LOYALISTS OF AMERICA AND THEIR TIMES, 1620-1816, Briggs, Toronto, Canada, 1880, 2 volumes.

___W. Brown, THE KING'S FRIENDS, Brown University Press, Providence, RI, 1966. [No lists.]

___W. Brown, THE GOOD AMERICANS, Morrow, New York, NY, 1969. [No lists.]

___R. M. Calhoon, THE LOYALISTS IN REVOLUTIONARY AMERICA, Harcourt Brace Jovanovich, New York, NY, 1973.

___P. R. N. Katcher, ENCYCLOPEDIA OF BRITISH, PROVINCIAL, AND GERMAN ARMY UNITS, 1775-83, Stackpole, Harrisburg, PA, 1973.

And the navy and naval operations are given extensive treatment in:

___G. W. Allen, A NAVAL HISTORY OF THE AMERICAN REVOLUTION, Corner House, Williamstown, MA, 1972.

___J. Coggins, SHIPS AND SEAMEN OF THE AMERICAN REVOLUTION, Stackpole Books, Harrisburg, PA, 1969.

___M. J. Smith, NAVIES IN THE AMERICAN REVOLUTION: A BIBLIOGRAPHY, Scarecrow Press, Metuchen, NJ, 1973.

___N. Miller, SEA OF GLORY: THE CONTINENTAL NAVY FIGHTS FOR INDEPENDENCE, 1775-83, McKay, New York, NY, 1973.

___N. Van Powell, THE AMERICAN NAVIES OF THE REVOLUTIONARY WAR, Putnam, New York, NY, 1974.

Not to be overlooked is a volume describing the part the marines played in the Revolution:

___C. R. Smith, MARINES IN THE REVOLUTION, History and Museums Division, US Marine Corps, Washington, DC, 1975.

The vital contributions made by blacks to practically all phases of the conflict are treated in these books:

___W. C. Nell, THE COLORED PATRIOTS OF THE AMERICAN REVOLUTION, Arno Press, New York, NY, 1968.

___P. S. Foner, BLACKS IN THE AMERICAN REVOLUTION, Greenwood, Westport, CT, 1975.

___H. Aptheker, THE NEGRO IN THE AMERICAN REVOLUTION, International, New York, NY, 1940.

___S. Kaplan, THE BLACK PRESENCE IN THE ERA OF THE AMERICAN REVOLUTION, Smithsonian, Washington, DC, 1973.

___B. Quarles, THE NEGRO IN THE AMERICAN REVOLUTION, University of NC Press, Chapel Hill, NC, 1961.

And the important assistance which women tendered during the seven years of strife is related in:

___S. S. Booth, THE WOMEN OF '76, Hastings, New York, NY, 1973. [No lists.]

___E. Evans, WEATHERING THE STORM: WOMEN OF THE AMERICAN REVOLUTION, Scribner's Sons, New York, NY, 1975.

___E. P. Meyer, PETTICOAT PATRIOTS OF THE REVOLUTION, Vanguard, Chicago, IL, 1978.

The nature of prisons and the deplorable conditions to which prisoners were subjected are described in:

__L. G. Bowman, CAPTIVE AMERICANS: PRISONERS DURING THE AMERICAN REVOLUTION, OH University Press, Athens, OH, 1976.

__C. H. Metzger, THE PRISONER IN THE AMERICAN REVOLUTION, Loyola University Press, Chicago, IL, 1971.

The important role that <u>German</u> troops played in the British effort to quell the Revolution is considered in:

__E. J. Lowell, THE HESSIANS AND OTHER GERMAN AUXILIARIES OF GREAT BRITAIN IN THE REVOLUTIONARY WAR, Harper, NY, 1884.

__M. von Eelking, THE GERMAN ALLIED TROOPS IN THE NORTH AMERICAN WAR OF INDEPENDENCE, Munsell, Albany, NY, 1893.

__H. Dippel, GERMANY AND THE AMERICAN REVOLUTION, University of NC Press, Chapel Hill, NC, 1977, pp. 19-45, 367-436. [Excellent list of sources in German and American archives.]

__P. R. N. Katcher, ENCYCLOPEDIA OF BRITISH, PROVINCIAL, AND GERMAN ARMY UNITS, 1775-83, Stackpole, Harrisburg, PA, 1973.

Many of the books listed above contain bibliographies which name numerous other works dealing with their subject matter.

7. Continental Army histories

Detailed treatments of the history of the Continental Army are available to those of you who wish to read further with regard to this subject. Among the more helpful of these are:

__F. A. Berg, ENCYCLOPEDIA OF CONTINENTAL ARMY UNITS, BATTALIONS, REGIMENTS, AND INDEPENDENT CORPS, Stackpole Books, Harrisburg, PA, 1972.

__H. H. Peckham, THE TOLL OF INDEPENDENCE, University of Chicago Press, Chicago, IL, 1974.

__C. K. Bolton, THE PRIVATE SOLDIER UNDER WASHINGTON, Scribner's, New York, NY, 1902.

__L. Montross, THE STORY OF THE CONTINENTAL ARMY, Barnes and Noble, New York, NY, 1952.

__H. L. Peterson, THE BOOK OF THE CONTINENTAL SOLDIER, Stackpole, Harrisburg, PA, 1968.

__C. Royster, A REVOLUTIONARY PEOPLE AT WAR, THE CONTINENTAL ARMY AND AMERICAN CHARACTER, University of NC Press, Chapel Hill, NC, 1979.

__A. Bowman, THE MORALE OF THE AMERICAN REVOLUTIONARY ARMY, Kennikat Press, Port Washington, NY, 1964.

__L. C. Hatch, ADMINISTRATION OF THE AMERICAN REVOLUTIONARY ARMY, Franklin, New York, NY, 1971.

Additional information, especially that contained in periodical articles, will be found listed in:

__R. W. Coakley and S. Conn, THE WAR OF THE AMERICAN REVOLUTION: NARRATIVE, CHRONOLOGY, AND BIBLIOGRAPHY, Center of Military History, US Army, Washington, DC, 1975.

8. Maps   As you make your way through the historical events of your Revolutionary War ancestor's life in the military service, it will often be of help to you to visualize certain events (particularly battles, troop movements, and ship journeys) on appropriate maps. There are several very good atlases available for your assistance. Notable among them are:

__L. J. Cappon and others, ATLAS OF EARLY AMERICAN HISTORY: THE REVOLUTIONARY ERA, 1760-90, Princeton University Press, Princeton, NJ, 1976.

__D. W. Marshall and H. H. Peckham, CAMPAIGNS OF THE AMERICAN REVOLUTION: AN ATLAS, Hammond, Maplewood, NY, 1975.

__K. Nebenzahl and D. Higginbotham, ATLAS OF THE AMERICAN REVOLUTION, Rand McNally, Chicago, IL, 1974.

__THE AMERICAN REVOLUTION, 1775-83, AN ATLAS, US Government Printing Office, Washington, DC, 1972.

__P. J. Guthorn, BRITISH MAPS OF THE AMERICAN REVOLUTION, Freneau, Monmouth Beach, NJ, 1972.

__P. J. Guthorn, AMERICAN MAPS AND MAP MAKERS IN THE REVOLUTION, Freneau, Monmouth Beach, NJ, 1966.

__E. D. Fite, A BOOK OF OLD MAPS DELINEATING AMERICAN HISTORY FROM THE EARLIEST TIMES DOWN TO THE CLOSE OF THE REVOLUTIONARY WAR, Dover, New York, NY, 1926.

__H. B. Carrington, BATTLE MAPS AND CHARTS OF THE AMERICAN REVOLUTION, Arno, New York, NY, 1881.

In addition to the above-mentioned atlases, there is an abundance of maps printed in books on the American Revolution and in periodical

articles dealing with the American War of Independence. Many of these
have been referenced and indexed in:

__D. S. Clark, INDEX TO MAPS OF THE AMERICAN
REVOLUTION IN BOOKS AND PERIODICALS, Greenwood,
Westport, CT, 1974.

Chapter 7

SITES, MUSEUMS, & MEMORIES

1. Introduction

In the process of delving deeper and deeper into your Revolutionary War ancestor's military career, you are likely to accumulate a great deal of information. Many of these data may deal with places your ancestor was (cities, towns, areas, camp sites, battle fields, river crossings, lakes, transportation centers, harbors). Other data will probably cause you to wonder about the uniforms he wore, the weapons he used, the equipment he carried, the tents hecamped in, the cities he attacked and/or retreated from, the food he ate, the hospitals he was treated in, the prisons he was held in, the earthworks from behind which he fought, and how he and his companions entertained themselves. There are a number of relics (or remains) of the American Revolution which will permit you to continue your investigations into these aspects of your veteran's military service. We will examine various relics (records, historic sites, museums, patriotic organizations) which you may want to pursue in quest of the surroundings and circumstances of your ancestor's military years.

2. Libraries

In many of the states of the US, particularly those which came from the 13 original colonies, you will find at least one library with a good to excellent collection of Revolutionary War books, microfilms, and sometimes even original documents. If your interest warrants it, you may plan to visit one or more of these libraries. Ask a librarian to assist you in examining the computer or card catalog for materials dealing with the subjects you are interested in. Also do not fail to go into the stacks and simply browse through the books in the Revolutionary War section and look at the labels on the microfilm cartons. In addition, you must not forget to ask if the library has a special section in which old Revolutionary War books and documents are housed.

It is well to bear in mind that even though any good Revolutionary War library will be of some assistance to you, the libraries nearer the places where your ancestor fought are more likely to have pertinent information. Names and locations of libraries with good to excellent Revolutionary War collections may be found in:

___M. L. and H. C. Young, DIRECTORY OF SPECIAL LIBRARIES, Gale Research Co., Detroit, MI, 1979.

___L. Ash, SUBJECT COLLECTIONS, Bowker, New York, NY, 1978.

If Revolutionary War records you have found indicate that your ancestor took part in a military action in or near a city, it is quite possible that the library in that city will have special records of the event. If the military action was in or near a village or a town, it is less likely that there will be local records, but it is a mistake not to inquire. Names and addresses of libraries in these cities, towns, and villages will be found in:
___AMERICAN LIBRARY DIRECTORY, Bowker, New York, NY, latest issue.
Don't forget to enclose an SASE when you write. And please remember, before travelling to visit any library, be sure and dispatch them an SASE and inquiry concerning whether they have records which might help you and what times they are open.

3. Historic sites Many organizations, both governmental and private, have identified, marked, preserved, beautified, and/or restored numerous historical sites associated with the Revolutionary War. A great deal of enjoyment can be had by visiting those with which your Revolutionary War ancestor was affiliated. In conjunction with some of these places there are libraries, displays, and/or museums. They are very valuable, so please don't overlook them.

Most of the historic sites that are worth visiting are called national military parks, national battlefields, national monuments, national historical parks, state parks, state memorial sites, county parks, DAR parks, private parks, or private historical sites. Included in them, as the titles indicate, are parks, battlegrounds, forts, monuments, earthworks, houses, and displays. In the tourist season, some of them, especially the nationally-sponsored ones, have battle reenactments and living displays.

In CT, the major site is:
___PUTNAM MEMORIAL STATE PARK, winter encampment of Continental Troops under Putnam in 1778-9, Redding, CT, [write CT Development Commission, 210 Washington St., Hartford, CT 06106].
In the state of FL are two notable sites:
___THOMAS CREEK BATTLEFIELD, where British forces held off Patriots from attacking St. Augustine in 1777, north of Jacksonville, FL, [write Department of Commerce, Collins Bldg., Tallahassee, FL 32304].
___CASTILLO DE SAN MARCOS NATIONAL MONUMENT, British

military base and prisoner center, [1 Castillo Dr., St. Augustine, FL 32084].

The most important of the GA sites is:

___BATTLE OF KETTLE CREEK SITE, maintained by the DAR, southwest of Washington, GA, in 1779 a Patriot victory here temporarily prevented Augusta from being occupied.

In MD, the best of the sites is:

___FORT FREDERICK STATE PARK, south of Clear Creek, MD, used for keeping British prisoners, [Division of Tourism, 2525 Riva Rd., Annapolis, MD 21401].

The state of MA provides several sites at which your ancestor may have been involved:

___BOSTON NATIONAL HISTORICAL PARK, Faneuil Hall, Old North Church, Old State House, Bunker Hill, Charles- town, Paul Revere House, [Charlestown Navy Yard, Boston, MA 02129].

___MINUTE MAN NATIONAL HISTORICAL PARK, North Bridge, Lexington-Concord Road, [PO Box 160, Concord, MA 01970].

___SALEM MARITIME NATIONAL HISTORIC SITE, old wharves, custom and warehouses, stores, [174 Derby St., Salem, MA 01970].

NJ also has quite a sizable array of historic sites related to the War of the Revolution:

___MORRISTOWN NATIONAL HISTORICAL PARK, winter head- quarters for the Continental Army, 1777 and 1779-80, [230 Morris St., Morristown, NJ 07960].

___WASHINGTON CROSSING STATE PARK, south of Titusville, NJ, where Washington crossed to attack Trenton, [State Promotion Office, Box 400, Trenton, NJ 08625].

___PRINCETON BATTLEFIELD STATE PARK, south edge of Prince- ton, NJ, [State Promotion Office, Box 400, Trenton, NJ 08625].

___MONMOUTH BATTLEFIELD STATE PARK, northwest of Freehold, NJ, [State Promotion Office, Box 400, Trenton, NJ 08625].

___RED BANK BATTLEFIELD COUNTY PARK, near town of National Park, NJ, battle fought in 1777 to block British supply lines, [State Promotion Office, Box 400, Trenton, NJ 08625].

In NY, the major sites include:

___FORT STANWIX NATIONAL MONUMENT, in Rome, NY, [112 E. Park St., Rome, NY 13440].

___SARATOGA NATIONAL HISTORICAL PARK, near Stillwater, NY, [R.D. 1, Box 113-C, Stillwater, NY 12170].

___FORT TICONDEROGA, restored fort, east of Ticonderoga, NY, under the management of a private corporation.

___MOUNT INDEPENDENCE, directly across lake from Fort Ticonderoga.

___BATTLE OF BENNINGTON STATE PARK, east of Waloomsac, NY, [NY Travel Bureau, 99 Washington Ave., Albany, NY 12210].

___ORISKANY BATTLEFIELD STATE PARK, between Oriskany and Rome, NY, [NY Travel Bureau, 99 Washington Ave., Albany, NY 12210].

___NEW WINDSOR CANTONMENT STATE HISTORIC SITE, Vails Gate, NY, [NY Travel Bureau, 99 Washington Ave., Albany, NY 12210].

Two sites of considerable note for NC may be mentioned:

___MOORES CREEK NATIONAL MILITARY PARK, near Currie, NC, [PO Box 69, Currie, NC 28435].

___GUILFORD COURTHOUSE NATIONAL MILITARY PARK, north of Greensboro, NC, [PO Box 9806, Greensboro, NC 27408].

For PA, the major sites include:

___INDEPENDENCE NATIONAL HISTORICAL PARK, in Philadelphia, PA, many important Revolutionary buildings such as Independence Hall, Congress Hall, old City Hall, and Franklin Hall, [313 Walnut St., Philadelphia, PA 19106].

___VALLEY FORGE NATIONAL HISTORICAL PARK, at Valley Forge, PA, [Valley Forge, PA 19481].

___WASHINGTON CROSSING STATE PARK, on the DE River in Bucks County, PA, [Bureau of Travel Development, South Office Bldg., Harrisburg, PA 17120].

The most important of the Revolutionary War sites in the state of RI is:

___NEWPORT HISTORIC DISTRICT, in Newport, RI, many historic buildings relating to the British, French, and American presences, [Tourist Promotion Division, 49 Hayes St., Providence, RI 02908].

In SC, several sites are to be considered:

___KINGS MOUNTAIN NATIONAL MILITARY PARK, just across the SC line south of Kings Mountain, NC, [PO Box 31, Kings Mountain, NC 28086].

___COWPENS NATIONAL BATTLEFIELD, east of Chesnee, SC, [PO Box 31, Kings Mountain, NC 28086].

___NINETY SIX NATIONAL HISTORIC SITE, at Ninety Six, SC, [PO Box 496, Ninety Six, SC 29666].

___CAMDEN BATTLEFIELD, north of Camden, SC, place of British defeat of Gates' Army in 1780, preserved by the DAR.

___EUTAW BATTLEFIELD STATE PARK, east of Eutawville, SC, site of 1781 defeat of British, leaving entire interior of SC in American hands, [SC Department of Tourism, PO Box 1358, Columbia, SC 29202].

One major Revolutionary War site in the state of <u>VT</u> needs to be drawn to your attention:

___HUBBARDTON BATTLEFIELD STATE PARK, east of Hubbardton, VT, site of surprise attack by British on rear guard of American force retreating from fall of Fort Ticonderoga, [Information and Travel Division, 63 Elm St., Montpelier, VT 05602].

The state of <u>VA</u> contains a couple of sites of note:

___COLONIAL NATIONAL HISTORICAL PARK, especially the surrender site at Yorktown, VA [PO Box 210, Yorktown, VA 23690].

___COLONIAL WILLIAMSBURG, INC., restoration of the Colonial town as it was in Revolutionary times, managed by a private corporation.

Not to be overlooked are three sites which were on the <u>Western Frontier</u> in the Revolutionary War years:

___GEORGE ROGERS CLARK NATIONAL HISTORICAL PARK, in Vincennes, IN, recognizes the winning of the Old Northwest Territory, [115 Dubois St., Vincennes, IN 47591].

___BLUE LICK SPRINGS STATE PARK, site of one of the last battles of the Revolution in which Indians ambushed and defeated an American force, at Blue Springs, KY, [KY Travel, Frankfort, KY 40601].

___PIONEER MEMORIAL STATE PARK, reconstruction of Revolutionary Fort Harrod where Clark planned his campaign of 1777-8, near Harrodsburg, KY, [KY Travel, Frankfort, KY 40601].

In addition to the many sites and sights mentioned above, there are literally hundreds more, all less elaborate than those above, but all being possible places where your ancestor was involved. There are four one-volume works which will guide you to quite a number of these sites:

___M. V. Alper, AMERICA'S FREEDOM TRAIL, Macmillan, New York, NY, 1980.

___J. V. Murfin, HISTORIC PLACES OF THE AMERICAN REVOLUTION, National Park Service, Washington, DC, 1975.

___M. M. Boatner, LANDMARKS OF THE AMERICAN REVOLUTION, Stackpole, Harrisburg, PA, 1973.

___H. D. Unrau, HERE WAS THE REVOLUTION, National Park Service, Washington, DC, 1976.

Even more sites are detailed in two multi-volumed guide books, both of which have extensive descriptive historical annotations:

___S. S. Bradford, LIBERTY'S ROAD: A GUIDE TO REVOLUTIONARY WAR SITES, McGraw-Hill, New York, NY, 1976, 2 volumes.

___S. Stember, THE BICENTENNIAL GUIDE TO THE AMERICAN REVOLUTION, Dutton, New York, NY, 1974, 3 volumes.

▄▄▄▄▄▄▄▄▄▄ As you continue your Revolutionary War research, one
4. Museums of the best ways to get a feel for the conditions under which your ancestor fought is to visit some of the many
▄▄▄▄▄▄▄▄▄▄ museums which have sizable collections of materials from the American Revolution. In these museums you will see weapons, uniforms, flags, insignia, camp furniture, cannons, vehicles, equipment, documents, saddles, and many other types of relics.

Among the most rewarding museums to pay a visit to are the following:

___In CT, JOSEPH WEBB HOUSE MUSEUM, Wethersfield, CT, operated by Colonial Dames.

___In DC, THE MUSEUM OF HISTORY AND TECHNOLOGY, Washington, DC, one of the topmost collections.

___In MA, BOSTON TEA PARTY MUSEUM, Boston, MA.

___In MA, STATE HOUSE, Beacon Hill, Boston, MA.

___In MA, FANEUIL HALL, Boston, MA.

___In MA, BUNKER HILL MONUMENT MUSEUM, Charlestown, MA.

___In NJ, MORRISTOWN NATIONAL HISTORICAL PARK MUSEUM, Morristown, NJ.

___In NJ, OLD BARRACKS MUSEUM, Trenton, NJ.

___In NY, SARATOGA NATIONAL HISTORICAL PARK MUSEUM, Stillwater, NY.

___In NY, NEW WINDSOR CANTONMENT STATE HISTORICAL SITE MUSEUM, Vails Gate, NY.

___In NY, FORT TICONDEROGA MUSEUM, Ticonderoga, NY.

___In NY, CROWN POINT STATE HISTORIC SITE MUSEUM, Crown Point, NY.

___In NY, FORT STANWIX MUSEUM, Rome, NY.

___In NY, BEAR MOUNTAIN HISTORICAL MUSEUM, Southfield, NY.

___In NY, WEST POINT MUSEUM, US MILITARY ACADEMY, West Point, NY.

___In NY, STONY POINT BATTLEFIELD STATE HISTORIC SITE

MUSEUM, Stony Point, NY.
___In <u>NY</u>, WASHINGTON'S HEADQUARTERS MUSEUM, New-burgh, NY.
___In <u>NY</u>, OLD STONE FORT, Schoharie, NY.
___In <u>NY</u>, FORT PLAIN MUSEUM, Fort Plain, NY.
___In <u>NC</u>, MOORES CREEK NATIONAL MILITARY PARK MUSEUM, Currie, NC.
___In <u>NC</u>, GUILFORD COURT HOUSE NATIONAL MILITARY PARK MUSEUM, Greensboro, NC.
___In <u>PA</u>, US ARMY MILITARY HISTORY INSTITUTE, Carlisle Barracks, PA.
___In <u>PA</u>, ARMY-NAVY MUSEUM, Philadelphia, PA.
___In <u>PA</u>, MARINE CORPS MUSEUM, Philadelphia, PA.
___In <u>SC</u>, KINGS MOUNTAIN NATIONAL MILITARY PARK MUSEUM, Blacksburg, SC.
___In <u>VA</u>, YORKTOWN VISITOR CENTER, Yorktown, VA.

Many other museums which have Revolutionary War displays are listed in:
___THE OFFICIAL MUSEUM DIRECTORY, The American Association of Museums, National Register, Skokie, IL, latest edition. This volume also gives brief descriptions of the collections in each museum it lists.

5. Patriotic organizations

There exist in the US quite a number of patriotic hereditary societies, including several which relate themselves to the American War for Independence. For membership, these latter oganizations require that a person prove a family connection to some Revolutionary War veteran or person who gave patriotic aid to the War effort. These societies keep records of the ancestral lineages which are presented to them by prospective members. They can often be very valuable to you in tracing your own War veteran or patriot and/or in connecting with lines leading to him or her. Several of them publish ancestor lists, membership lists, and/or lineage books. The most widely known of these organizations is the National Society of the Daughters of the American Revolution (DAR), their state societies, and their approximately 3000 local chapters. This society has about 200,000 members, and they maintain a 60,000- item library in Washington, DC. Their members have been and continue to be very active in collecting, indexing, and publishing genealogical records, especially those dealing with the American Revolution. You have undoubtedly noticed many of their publications as you have read previous chapters in this book and as you have investigated your forebears. To become a member, a woman over 18 years of age must prove that she is a direct lineal descendant of a person who gave unfailing loyalty and military or public service to the American cause. The address of the society is:

___The National Society of the Daughters of the American Revolution, 1776 D St., NW, Washington, DC 20008.

Among other patriotic hereditary societies is the National Society of the Sons of the Revolution (SAR). This organization of over 20,000 men requires their members to be men over 18 who prove that they are lineal descendants of a person who showed unfailing loyalty to the Revolutionary cause and rendered either military or public service aimed at overthrow of the British authority. They have chapters in all 50 of the states of the US. Addresses of the state branches may be found in:

___V. N. Chambers, editor, THE GENEALOGICAL HELPER, Everton Publishers, Logan, UT, latest Jul-Aug issue.

The address of the national headquarters is:

___The National Society of the Sons of the American Revolution, 1000 S. Fourth St., Louisville, KY 40203.

The Society of the Cincinnati was organized in 1783 for veterans who had been commissioned officers in the Continental Army and had served for 3 years or until the surrender or had been disabled or killed or died in service. Membership was then extended to the officer's eldest male descendant, and then to lineal or collateral male descendants. The organization has a book of about 2400 officers to whom one must trace himself in order to qualify for membership. The organization, which takes its name from the Roman citizen-soldier Lucius Quintus Cincinnatus, has the following address:

___The Society of the Cincinnati, 2118 Massachusetts Ave., NW, Washington, DC 20008.

The city of Cincinnati, OH, was named in honor of the society. There is an organization similar to the Society of the Cincinnati which is made up of female descendants of officers of the Continental Army:

___Daughters of the Cincinnati, 122 East 58th St., New York, NY 10022.

Other organizations which require lineal descent or specified patriotic service in the Revolution include:

___The General Society of Sons of the Revolution, Fraunces Tavern, 54 Pearl St., New York, NY 10004 [men over 21].

___The National Society of Children of the American Revolution, 1776 D

St., NW, Washington, DC 20006 [boys and girls under 21].
___The National Society of Daughters of the Revolution of 1776, 701 Dryden Dr., Baltimore, MD 21229 [women over 18].
Two societies, one for men and one for women, require lineal descent from a person who settled in what is now the US during 1607-87, and the line must include an ancestor who gave military or civil service to the Revolutionary War effort:
___The National Society of the Daughters of Founders and Patriots of America, 1307 New Hampshire Ave., NW, Washington, DC 20036 [women over 18].
___The Order of the Founders and Patriots of America, 53 State St., Boston, MA 02109 [men 18 and over].
There is also an organization made up of persons who are descended from soldiers and other patriots who were camped with Washington at Valley Forge in the winter-spring of 1777-8:
___Society of the Descendants of Washington's Army at Valley Forge, PO Box 608, Manhasset, NY 11030.
A very interesting organization is The Hereditary Order of Descendants of the Loyalists and Patriots of the American Revolution. To be eligible for membership, a man or woman must demonstrate descent from both an American patriot and from a Loyalist ancestor. The address is:
___The Hereditary Order of Descendants of the Loyalists and Patriots of the American Revolution, 1307 New Hampshire Ave., NW, Washington, DC 20036.
A volume which lists numerous hereditary and patriotic societies and gives details on each (including those listed above) is:
___J. G. R. Rountree, THE HEREDITARY REGISTER OF THE USA, Hereditary Register, Washington, DC, 1973.

Some of the publications of some of these organizations which have not heretofore been taken note of are as follows. In a few instances, they can provide you with data not available elsewhere.
___National Society of the Daughters of Founders and Patriots of America, LINEAGE BOOKS, The Society, Washington, DC, 1910-, vol. 1-, to be used with INDEX TO LINEAGE BOOKS: VOLUMES 1-25, The Society, Somerville, MA, 1943, and with FOUNDERS AND PATRIOTS INDEX: VOLUMES 1-34, The Society, Washington, DC, 1975.
___L. H. Cornish and A. H. Clarke, A NATIONAL REGISTER, Sons of the American Revolution, New York, NY, 1902.
___The Order of the Founders and Patriots of America, REGISTER, The Order, New York, NY, 1926; FIRST SUPPLEMENT, 1940; SECOND

SUPPLEMENT, 1960.

6. Personal book collection

If it turns out that you want to extend your research to the Revolutionary War careers of the brothers of your fifth or sixth great grandfathers and those of the brothers of your fifth or sixth great grandmothers, it is recommended that you build up a core library of Revolutionary War volumes to facilitate your work. Listed below are the books which could save you much travel to libraries:

__(a) G. B. Everton, Sr., HANDY BOOK FOR GENEALOGISTS, Everton Publishers, Logan, UT, 1982.

__(b) Geo. K. Schweitzer, GENEALOGICAL SOURCE HANDBOOK, $15 postpaid from Geo. K. Schweitzer at the address given on the title page of this book.

__(c) R. M. Ketchum, THE AMERICAN HERITAGE BOOK OF THE REVOLUTION, American Heritage, New York, NY, 1958.

__(d) J. R. Alden, A HISTORY OF THE AMERICAN REVOLUTION, Knopf, New York, NY, 1969.

__(e) M. M. Boatner, ENCYCLOPEDIA OF THE AMERICAN REVOLUTION, McKay, New York, NY, 1966.

__(f) R. W. Coakley and S. Conn, THE WAR OF THE AMERICAN REVOLUTION: NARRATIVE, CHRONOLOGY, AND BIBLIOGRAPHY, Center of Military History, US Army, Washington, DC, 1975.

__(g) J. V. Murfin, HISTORIC PLACES OF THE AMERICAN REVOLUTION, National Park Service, Washington, DC, 1975.

__(h) National DAR, DAR PATRIOT INDEX, The Society, Washington, DC, 1966, 1979, 2 volumes.

__(i) National Genealogical Society, INDEX OF REVOLUTIONARY WAR PENSION APPLICATIONS IN THE NATIONAL ARCHIVES, The Society, Washington, DC, 1976.

__(j) M. E. Deutrich and H. H. Wehmann, PRELIMINARY INVENTORY OF THE WAR DEPARTMENT COLLECTION OF REVOLUTIONARY WAR RECORDS, National Archives, Washington, DC, 1970.

__(k) J. C. and L. L. Neagles, LOCATING YOUR REVOLUTIONARY WAR ANCESTOR, Everton Publishers, Logan, UT, 1983.

Book (a) is a basic genealogical tool listing all the counties in the US, their county seats, their county seat addresses, their records officials, their vital record and land record holdings, plus general genealogi- cal data for each state. Book (b) is a practical guidebook to genealogical research listing all major plus many minor genealogical information sources with precise details and exact instructions for obtaining the information. Book (c) is an excellent, beautifully illustrated, one-volume history of the Revolutionary War which will give you a broad overview of the sequence of events that will permit you to place your Revolutionary ancestor in the stream of occurrences. Book (d) is one of the best standard scholarly histories of the War which will provide added interpretive detail to your knowledge. Book (e) is a one-volume encyclopedia which gives brief articles on events, leaders, and sites associated with the War, and then guides you to further details. Book (f) is valuable for its detailed chronology of the events of the War and its detailed bibliography of books and periodical articles dealing with various aspects of the conflict. Book (g) is a guide to Revolutionary War campaign and battle sites which gives you locations of battlegrounds, monuments,, museums, and houses along with brief statements of what you should see at each. If you plan to do extensive visiting of such places, you might purchase instead one of the three other books listed in the section on historic sites (section 3 of this chapter). Books (h) and (i) are extensive listings of Revolutionary War soldiers, sailors, marines, and patriots plus pension applications of veterans, widows, and heirs. Book (j) is a detailed listing of the vast Revolutionary War records available to you in the National Archives. Many of these records have scarcely been touched by genealogical researchers. Book (k) is a very detailed guide to the vast store of federal, state, and local Revolutionary War records available in a wide variety of repositories.

7. Books and bookshops

Most volumes on the American Revolution which are in print are available through any standard bookstore who will be willing to order for you. Almost all such stores will have a copy of the basic reference work which lists most in-print books:

___BOOKS IN PRINT, Author, Title, and Subject Guides, Bowker, New York, NY, 6 volumes, latest issue.

If, therefore, you want to purchase a certain book on the Revolutionary War, you should first find out if the book is in print by consulting the above reference volume at your bookstore or in a library. There are three other works that can be quite helpful to you for locating books. The first of these lists older books which have been reprinted. There are many such books in both the genealogical and Revolutionary War categories. This work is:

___GUIDE TO REPRINTS AND SUBJECT GUIDE TO REPRINTS,

Guide to Reprints, Kent, CT, 4 volumes, latest issue.
The <u>second</u> is an extensive listing of books and documents which have
been made available on microfilm. This list is found in:

__GUIDE TO MICROFORMS IN PRINT, Subject, Author, and Title
    Listings, Microform Review, Westport, CT, 2 volumes, latest issue.
The <u>third</u> reference work is a listing of rare books which a company will
photocopy for you. This volume is entitled:

__BOOKS ON DEMAND, Author, Subject, and Title Guides, University
    Microfilms, Ann Arbor, MI, 3 volumes, latest issue.
All of the above volumes should be consulted as you seek to purchase
books relating to your ancestor and his Revolutionary War activities. The
last three of them are usually found in larger bookstores and larger
libraries.

When you want to purchase books relating to the American War of
Independence, you will find that your needs can be efficiently met if you
deal with one of the many book stores which specialize in Revolutionary
War volumes. They usually have or have access to all the reference
volumes discussed in the previous paragraph, and they will use them in
seeking to find a book you asked for. However, where the specialty
bookstores really can be indispensible are for cases in which you need to
purchase an out-of-print volume. They maintain an information network
which permits them to make nationwide searches for such books. To
locate such bookstores in your vicinity, consult the following work which
you will find in most medium-sized and large libraries:

__AMERICAN BOOK TRADE DIRECTORY, Bowker, New York,
    NY, latest edition.
Look in it under your state, then locate your city, and/or cities near you,
and under them, identify the bookstores which are designated as
antiquarian.

Books by George K. Schweitzer

CIVIL WAR GENEALOGY. A 93-paged book of 316 sources for tracing your Civil War ancestor. Chapters include I: The Civil War, II: The Archives, III: National Publications, IV: State Publications, V: Local Sources, VI: Military Unit Histories, VII: Civil War Events.

GEORGIA GENEALOGICAL RESEARCH. A 238-paged book containing 1303 sources for tracing your GA ancestor along with detailed instructions. Chapters include I: GA Background, II: Types of Records, III: Record Locations, IV: Research Procedure and County Listings (detailed listing of records available for each of the 159 GA counties).

HANDBOOK OF GENEALOGICAL SOURCES. A 252-paged book describing all major and many minor sources of genealogical information with precise and detailed instructions for obtaining data from them.

INDIANA GENEALOGICAL RESEARCH. A 189-paged book containing 1044 sources for tracing your IN ancestor along with detailed instructions. Chapters include I: IN Background, II: Types of Records, III: Record Locations, IV: Research Procedure and County Listings (detailed listing of records available for each of the 92 IN counties).

KENTUCKY GENEALOGICAL RESEARCH. A 167-paged book containing 1191 sources for tracing your KY ancestor along with detailed instructions. Chapters include I: KY Background, II: Types of Records, III: Record Locations, IV: Research Procedure and County Listings (detailed listing of records available for each of the 120 KY counties).

MARYLAND GENEALOGICAL RESEARCH. A 208-paged book containing 1176 sources for tracing your MD ancestor along with detailed instructions. Chapters include I: MD Background, II: Types of Records, III: Record Locations, IV: Research Procedure and County Listings (detailed listing of records available for each of the 23MD counties and for Baltimore City).

MASSACHUSETTS GENEALOGICAL RESEARCH. A 279-paged book containing 1709 sources for tracing your MA ancestor along with detailed instructions. Chapters include I: MA Background, II: Types of Records, III: Record Locations, IV: Research Procedure and County-Town-City Listings (detailed listing of records available for each of the 14 MA counties and the 351 cities-towns).

NEW YORK GENEALOGICAL RESEARCH. A 252-paged book containing 1426 sources for tracing your NY ancestor along with detailed instructions. Chapters include I: NY Background, II: Types of Records, III: Record Locations, IV: Research Procedure and NY City Record Listings (detailed listing of records available for the 5 counties of NY City), V: Record Listings for Other Counties (detailed listing of records available for each of the other 57 NY counties).

NORTH CAROLINA GENEALOGICAL RESEARCH. A 169-paged book containing 1233 sources for tracing your NC ancestor along with detailed instructions. Chapters include I: NC Background, II: Types of Records, III: Record Locations, IV: Research Procedure and County Listings (detailed listing of records available for each of the 100 NC counties).

OHIO GENEALOGICAL RESEARCH. A 212-paged book containing 1241 sources for tracing your OH ancestor along with detailed instructions. Chapters include I: OH Background, II: Types of Records, III: Record Locations, IV: Research Procedure and County Listings (detailed listing of records available for each of the 100 OH counties).

PENNSYLVANIA GENEALOGICAL RESEARCH. A 201-paged book containing 1309 sources for tracing your PA ancestor along with detailed instructions. Chapters include I: PA Background, II: Types of Records, III: Record Locations, IV: Research Procedure and County Listings (detailed listing of records available for each of the 67 PA counties).

REVOLUTIONARY WAR GENEALOGY. A 110-paged book containing 407 sources for tracing your Revolutionary War ancestor. Chapters include I: Revolutionary War History, II: The Archives, III: National Publications, IV: State Publications, V: Local Sources, VI: Military Unit Histories, VII: Sites and Museums.

SOUTH CAROLINA GENEALOGICAL RESEARCH. A 170-paged book containing 1107 sources for tracing your SC ancestor along with detailed instructions. Chapters include I: SC Background, II: Types of Records, III: Record Locations, IV: Research Procedure and County Listings (detailed listing of records available for each of the 47 SC counties and districts).

TENNESSEE GENEALOGICAL RESEARCH. A 132-paged book containing 1073 sources for tracing your TN ancestor along with detailed instructions. Chapters include I: TN Background, II: Types of Records, III: Record Locations, IV: Research Procedure and County Listings (detailed listing of records available for each of the 96 TN counties).

VIRGINIA GENEALOGICAL RESEARCH. A 216-paged book containing 1273 sources for tracing your VA ancestor along with detailed instructions. Chapters include I: VA Background, II: Types of Records, III: Record Locations, IV: Research Procedure and County Listings (detailed listing of records available for each of the 100 VA counties and 41 major cities).

WAR OF 1812 GENEALOGY. A 75-paged book of 289 sources for tracing your War of 1812 ancestor. Chapters include I: History of the War, II: Service Records, III: Bounty Land and Pension Records, IV: National and State Publications, V: Local Sources, VI: Military Unit Histories, VII: Sites and Events.

All of the above books may be ordered from Dr. George K. Schweitzer at the address given on the title page. Or send a long SASE for a FREE descriptive leaflet.